Mark Williams is Emeritus Professor of Clinical Psychology at Oxford University. He co-developed mindfulness-based cognitive therapy (MBCT), is co-author of the international bestseller *Mindfulness: Finding Peace in a Frantic World*, and *The Mindful Way Through Depression* and author of *Cry of Pain: Understanding Suicide and the Suicidal Mind*.

Dr Danny Penman is a meditation teacher and award-winning writer and journalist. He is co-author of the bestseller *Mindfulness: Finding Peace in a Frantic World*. In 2014, he jointly won the British Medical Association's Best Book (Popular Medicine) Award for *Mindfulness for Health: A Practical Guide to Relieving Pain, Reducing Stress and Restoring Wellbeing*. His books have been translated into more than 30 languages. He has received journalism awards from the RSPCA and the Humane Society of the United States, and his work has appeared in the *Daily Mail*, the *Guardian*, the *Telegraph*, and *New Scientist*. He has also researched and produced documentaries for the BBC and Channel 4. He holds a PhD in biochemistry.

Deeper Mindfulness

The new way to
REDISCOVER CALM
IN A CHAOTIC WORLD

MARK WILLIAMS
AND DANNY PENMAN

PIATKUS

PIATKUS

First published in Great Britain in 2023 by Piatkus

1 3 5 7 9 10 8 6 4 2

Copyright © Mark Williams and Danny Penman 2023

The moral right of the authors has been asserted.

'Spacious' by Kaveri Patel © Kaveri Patel. Reproduced with permission.

A CIP catalogue record for this book
is available from the British Library.

ISBN 978-0-349-43320-2

Typeset in Sabon by M Rules
Printed and bound in Great Britain by
Clays Ltd, Elcograf S.p.A

Papers used by Piatkus are from well-managed forests
and other responsible sources.

MIX
Supporting
responsible forestry
FSC® C104740

Piatkus
An imprint of
Little, Brown Book Group
Carmelite House
50 Victoria Embankment
London EC4Y 0DZ

An Hachette UK Company
www.hachette.co.uk

www.littlebrown.co.uk

The personal stories shared in this book are based on the
experiences of those who have followed the programme;
however, the names of all participants and some details of
their stories have been changed to preserve anonymity.

Dedication

DANNY
To Sasha and Luka

MARK
To Elliot and Sebastian

CONTENTS

CHAPTER ONE

That Was My Life ... But I Must Have Missed It

Every morning, a man walked his four dogs in the park. Three of them always darted about, barking happily, tails wagging with delight. The fourth seemed happy enough but would only ever run around in tight little circles (albeit covering quite a distance), staying close to the man as he walked. Day after day, the park keeper watched the dog's strange behaviour. After a while, the keeper plucked up the courage to ask the man why his dog was behaving so oddly.[1]

'Ah,' the man replied. 'She's a rescue dog. She was locked up for most of her life. That was the size of her cage.'

How often have you behaved like that dog? Free, but constantly running around in little mental circles. Free to be happy, yet caged by the same dark, repetitive thoughts. Free to be at peace with yourself and the world, while remaining trapped and entangled by anxiety, stress, unhappiness and exhaustion.

Free as a dog in a cage.

So much of life is needlessly marred by little tragedies such as these. Deep down, we all know that we are capable of living happy and fulfilling lives, and yet something always stops us from doing so. Just as life seems to be within our grasp, it slips through our fingers. Although such periods of distress seem to appear from nowhere, they actually arise from deeply buried psychological forces. Neuroscientists have begun to understand how these processes guide our thoughts, feelings and emotions; but more importantly, they have discovered why they occasionally go wrong and leave our lives as shadows of their true potential. These new discoveries also show why mindfulness is so effective at relieving distress, but crucially, they also open the door to subtly different methods that can be even more effective. Mindfulness has not been superseded; rather, it can be expanded to include an extra dimension that transforms it.

This is a book that harnesses these new developments. It will help you to step aside from your worries and give you the tools necessary to deal with anxiety, stress, unhappiness, exhaustion and even depression. And when these unpleasant emotions evaporate, you will rediscover a calm space inside from which you can rebuild your life.

We can help you to do this because we – and our colleagues at Oxford University and other institutions around the world – have spent many years developing treatments for anxiety, stress, depression and exhaustion. We co-developed Mindfulness-based Cognitive Therapy (MBCT), which has been clinically proven to be one of the most effective treatments for depression so far developed.[2] Out of this work arose our book *Mindfulness:*

Finding Peace in a Frantic World. That book, and the mind-fulness programme within it, has been proven in clinical trials at Cambridge University and elsewhere to be a highly effective treatment for anxiety, stress and depression. So much so, that it is prescribed by doctors and psychiatrists around the world to help people cope with a wide range of mental-health conditions, as well as generalised unhappiness and dissatisfaction with life.

But the practices revealed in *Mindfulness*, and similar skills taught on courses such as Mindfulness-based Stress Reduction (MBSR), are only the first steps on a longer and more fruitful road. Although they form the foundations for a happier and more fulfilling life, and have proven transformative for many, a lot of people have asked us whether there is anything more they could do to enhance their practice and resolve their remaining issues.

The answer is *yes*. There is a way of taking mindfulness to the next level, of going deeper and unleashing more of your potential, by exploring another frontier of mindfulness known as *vedana* or *feeling tone*. And, importantly, you don't need to have extensive meditation experience to benefit from these practices. Research is showing that novice meditators can gain just as much from them as those who have practised for many years.

Although it is an often-overlooked aspect of meditation, feeling tone is, in fact, one of the four original foundations of mindfulness. These are: mindfulness of the body and breath; mindfulness of feelings and sensations (or vedana); mindfulness of the mind or consciousness; and mindfulness of the ever-changing nature of the world and what helps and hinders your journey through it. Each aspect is cultivated using a different set of practices that, together, bring about profoundly different effects on mind and body. Mindfulness courses generally focus on the first layer of each of these four foundations. This book uses new meditations on feeling tone as a gateway into the deeper layers of the same four aspects of mindfulness. These take you closer to the source of your 'spirit'; closer to any difficulties you may be having; nearer still to their resolution.

There is no satisfactory translation of the ancient Sanskrit word *vedana*.[3]

It is a quality of awareness that can only be experienced, not pinned down with precision. It is the feeling, almost a background 'colour', that tinges our experience of the world – of mindfulness itself. For this reason, vedana is often translated as *feeling tone*. Although we will use both terms interchangeably, it will always pay to remember that we are referring to a flavour of awareness, and not a rigid concept that can be hedged in by words and definitions. Feeling tone is something that you feel in mind, body and 'spirit', but its true quality will always remain slightly ineffable. Sometimes annoyingly so.

A typical feeling-tone meditation consists of stilling the mind with a simple breath or body meditation and then paying attention to your experiences in a manner that is subtly different to what other meditations request. It asks you to focus in a very specific way on the feelings and sensations that arise in the moment when the unconscious mind crystallises into the conscious one. Such moments, though fleeting, are often the most important ones in your life. This is because vedana is the balance point in your mind that sets the tone for the sequence of thoughts, feelings and emotions that follow. It is often subtle, but if you pay attention to it, you can feel it in your mind, body and spirit – right through to your bones. The feeling tone is of profound importance because it guides the trajectory of your subsequent thoughts, feelings and emotions. If it is 'pleasant', you will tend to feel positive, dynamic and in control of your life (at least for a while). If it is 'unpleasant', you will likely feel slightly gloomy, deflated and powerless. Feeling-tone meditations teach you to see, or more precisely, to *feel* the way that your life is pushed and pulled around by forces you are barely conscious of. Sometimes these forces act in your best interests, sometimes not – but the important thing is that they are not under your immediate control. Under their influence, your life is not your own.

To help these ideas settle into your mind, you might like to try this little practice to get a sense of your feeling tones: if it is convenient, take a few moments to look around you; the room, the window, the interior of your train or bus, or perhaps the street, field or forest before you. As your eyes alight on different things, or different sounds come to your ears, see if you can register the subtle sense of whether each one feels pleasant, unpleasant or neutral. If you are at home, your eye might alight on a card, gift or memento from a much-loved friend. You might feel the instant warm glow of a pleasant feeling tone in response. Or you might see a dirty dish that you've been meaning to tidy away, or something you've borrowed from someone and had intended to return, and then you might notice an unpleasant feeling tone. If you are outside, you may notice the sun streaming through the leaves of a tree, or a piece of dirty plastic rubbish flapping around. If you can catch the moment, you might sense ripples of pleasant or unpleasant feeling tones. But it is not just the external world that has such an impact. You may also become aware of sensations inside your body, such as aches and pains, or perhaps a sense of relaxed calm. These, too, register on the same dimension of pleasant, unpleasant or neutral. And sooner or later, you may notice thoughts or emotions arising and passing away soon after the feeling tones.

You don't need to know *how* you know these feeling tones – you just know. Somehow there is a 'read-out' in body and mind on the dimension of pleasant to unpleasant. It's like a gut feeling. It's not a matter of thinking hard about it, or hunting for it, it's more like the taste of something; you just know it when you taste it. Like tasting milk that's gone sour, you know it's unpleasant without having to think about it.

Feeling tones can be hugely significant. Cast your mind back to the last time you were sitting in a café and suddenly felt unhappy for no apparent reason. If you could rewind the clock and observe what was happening – frame by frame – as your unhappiness arose, you would have noticed that the emotion was preceded by a momentary pause. It was as if your mind was poised on a knife-edge, a moment when it was sensing whether the evolving situation was *pleasant*, *unpleasant* or *neutral*. A moment of vedana.

So vedana is often a tipping point in your mind that affects how you experience the world in the moments that follow. Good, bad, indifferent. But it is what happens next that is of paramount importance – we call it 'the reactivity pulse'. It works like this: if a pleasant feeling tone arises in the mind, then it is entirely natural to want to grasp it, keep hold of it and be a little fearful that it will fade away or slip through your fingers. If the tone is unpleasant, then it is natural to want to get rid of it, to push it away, fearing that it will stick around for ever and never leave. Neutral sensations often feel boring, so you feel like tuning out and finding something more interesting to do. These feeling tones are primal and can quickly trigger a cascade of reactions in the mind and body. These are felt as emotions and cravings that compel you to try to keep hold of pleasant feeling tones, push away unpleasant ones and distract yourself from neutral ones. So, the reactivity pulse is the mind's knee-jerk reaction to feeling tone. If a feeling tone sets the scene, then the reactivity pulse casts the actors, selects the costumes and writes the script for what happens next. And it can write a script and direct a scene that can easily ruin your whole day and sometimes far, far, longer.

Virtually all of the emotional difficulties that many of us experience begin with the mind's reaction to our feeling tones – our reactivity pulse. But it's not even the pulse itself that is the problem, but our ignorance of its existence and underlying nature. We are often not aware that it has occurred, oblivious of the feeling tone that triggered it and unaware of its tendency to fade away, all by itself, if only we would allow it to do so. All we are aware of is the cascade of thoughts, feelings and emotions that follow in its wake.

Learning to sense the feeling tone – bringing it into the light – teaches you to recognise your underlying state of mind and helps you make allowances for your sensitivities and entirely natural biases and reactions. It gives you the space to respond rather than react. It helps you to compassionately accept that although you might be anxious, stressed, angry or depressed in *this* moment, this is not the totality of your life with only one depressing future ahead of you. You can change course. Alternative futures are available to you.

And tapping into an alternative future is as simple as sensing the underlying flow of feeling tones. Noticing the reactivity pulses. Realising that the craving for things to be different *is* the problem. Craving an end to unpleasantness. Craving for pleasantness to remain. Craving an end to boredom. This idea is common to many ancient traditions. And now, neuro-science agrees.

Why cultivate awareness of the feeling tone of your thoughts, memories and emotions?

Your thoughts, feelings, memories and emotions are not the problem, no matter how unpleasantly real and visceral they might feel. As an example, emotions are signals that something important needs our attention:

- We feel sad if we've lost something or someone important.
- We feel fear when a threat appears on the horizon.
- We feel angry when a goal is thwarted.
- We are preoccupied when a long-term project needs our problem-solving skills.

In many ways, the real problem is the reactivity pulse (see page 6), triggered by fluctuations in the underlying feeling tone. This creates a narrative so compelling that we can get stuck inside our thoughts, feelings, emotions and memories and can't escape.

Learning to sense the feeling tone that precedes this reactivity pulse gives you extra information. It signals to you the very moment when your thoughts, feelings, emotions or memories are likely to seize control, become entangled and spiral out of control. This programme teaches you how to recognise these moments so you can step in and dissolve your old, destructive habits. It will help you rediscover the calm, vigour and joy that lie at the core of your being.

HOW CAN THIS BOOK HELP YOU?

Our previous book, *Mindfulness: Finding Peace in a Frantic World*, became the 'go-to' book for so many people because it helped them find freedom from their emotional and physical suffering. Throughout the book, we were honest about the benefits of mindfulness, and also warned readers that their journey would not be quick or particularly easy. We asked them to be certain that they were at the right moment in their life to begin, and highlighted that they would need to set aside the necessary time each day to actually do the practices. Despite these caveats, hundreds of thousands of people – perhaps millions – completed the programme in the book (or mindfulness courses based upon it). Many of these people became so intrigued by the effects of meditation on their lives that they wanted to broaden and deepen their practice. Perhaps you are one of them. If you, like them, would like to go beyond the eight-week programme taught in *Mindfulness*, or on your meditation, MBCT or MBSR course, and extend your practice to embed its benefits, this book is a good place for you to begin.

Alternatively, you may have found *Mindfulness*, or a course, helpful but it did not go far enough to completely dissolve your remaining negative or self-destructive habits. Perhaps you caught a glimpse of freedom but then lost it once again in your rush through life and now want to renew your acquaintance with it. Or, maybe, the mindfulness skills you learned on courses or through books didn't quite 'gel' with you and you now want to try a different approach. If any of these is true for you, then this book will likely help you.

In *Deeper Mindfulness*, and the accompanying meditation

downloads, we reveal the Feeling Tone programme. This is not simply a sequel to our original book, or to other meditation courses and classes; rather, it is one that will take your practice in a new and even more fruitful direction. And if you don't have any meditation experience, there is no reason to be put off. The programme has been found to be equally helpful for both novice and experienced meditators, especially for those seeking a practice that combines scientific rigour with millennia-old wisdom.

If you are keen to start this new meditation programme straight away, we suggest that you turn to Chapter Four after reading this chapter. If you would first like to know more about the ideas underpinning the programme, start with Chapters Two and Three. The practice of becoming aware of feeling tone, like mindfulness in general, is enhanced if you understand how and why the different meditations work. It is also useful (and fascinating) to know at the deepest of levels how the mind works and how, occasionally, we can begin suffering from anxiety, stress, depression, exhaustion and a host of other problems. Whether you read these chapters first or as you work through the programme, you will find that they greatly enhance it. The final eight chapters of the book (five to twelve) contain the week-by-week programme.

We wish you well on your journey.

The links to the accompanying meditations can be found in the 'Practices for the week' boxes in Chapters five to twelve. We suggest that you read through the written meditation instructions as you come to them in the book before listening to the audio versions and following their guidance.

CHAPTER TWO

Why Do We Exhaust Ourselves?

Zoe was staring blankly at the computer screen. Stuck. She's the team leader in the office of an enormous 'fulfilment centre' run by an online clothing retailer. As she freely admits, there's nothing fulfilling about working in the warehouse. The company demands perfection, which is often at odds with its other stated aims of speed and efficiency. And with it expanding so fast, there are never enough people to do all that is required, meaning that Zoe is often forced to do others' jobs in parallel to her own. Which is just the way everyone (except Zoe) likes it. Zoe is so efficient that many of her colleagues turn to her whenever there's a problem, rather than sorting it out for themselves. In the past, this made Zoe feel important. Now she's just jaded and short-tempered. She's also begun procrastinating endlessly, rather like an overloaded computer prone to freezing. Such episodes of grumpy mental blankness have started happening increasingly often and are getting progressively worse, as she finds herself thinking, *Oh, God, this should be easy. Why the hell do they keep changing things? I just can't keep up any more. Maybe it's me? I'm just not as fast as I used to be. Or as clever. Everything is so rushed. Why am I so tired all the time? No wonder I don't have a life ... I just don't have the time or energy to juggle everything ... too tired to cope.*

Zoe took another gulp of the strong coffee that the company gave away by the gallon. The phone rang. It was her boss demanding that she reschedule that afternoon's two o'clock meeting. This meant reorganising schedules for six other people. A red banner appeared on screen – the warehouse team was behind schedule and needed the office staff to help them pick and pack items for delivery. She reached for the tannoy to make the announcement. At which point, her daughter Megan's primary school rang. Megan had a high temperature, so Zoe would have to go and collect her early. Except that her car was in the garage for repairs and would not be ready until later that afternoon. 'Oh, for God's sake,' she cursed under her breath. Her mind blanked out and she glanced out of the window to the warehouse floor. Dinky tank-tracked robots scurried about, picking and packing orders. *They're getting to be as good as us now*, she thought. *And the only ones left alone long enough to actually concentrate on their work.*

Then she remembered that the warehouse had been reorganised overnight; the human workers were now helping the robots to do *their* work. Her heart sank a little further. Such fears for the future were becoming a central part of Zoe's life and were starting to keep her awake at night: *It's only going to get worse. How will our children cope? There simply won't be the jobs, let alone good ones. They won't even be able to get a flat of their own, certainly not a house. All the money will be in the hands of the tech barons; we'll just get a few crumbs from the table. No more than rats to those at the top ...* It was getting to the point where a couple of big glasses of wine were needed to relax Zoe enough for sleep.

Zoe's story is hardly unique. She's overworked and her life has been taken over by anxiety and a gnawing sense of unhappiness. She desperately wants to be happy, to have enough time and energy for herself and her young family, but she has no idea how to get there. She's not anxious, stressed or depressed in a clinical sense, nor has she 'burned out', but neither is she energised and truly happy. She's existing rather than living.

If you asked Zoe to tease apart what was happening in her mind when she was 'rushed and stressed out', she would realise that the relentless demands of work combined with her hectic pace of life were overloading her mind and driving it around in circles. Her constant activity might make her look efficient, but inside she was crumbling. This is hardly surprising. Trying to juggle too many demands at once exacts a significant but largely hidden price. Try this little exercise to see why:

Time yourself while you recite the first two lines of this nursery rhyme:

Mary had a little lamb,
Its fleece was white as snow.

How long did it take to say these eleven words? About four seconds?

> Now time yourself while you count to eleven.
>
> Four seconds again? So, it takes about eight seconds to recite the two lines of verse and then count to eleven.
>
> Now time yourself as you close your eyes and alternate between saying the words of the nursery rhyme and the numbers. That is: Mary-1; had-2; a-3 and so on.
>
> How long does this take? Around sixteen to twenty seconds?

The additional time it takes to alternate between the words of the nursery rhyme and the numbers one to eleven is the so-called 'switching cost'. It takes more time because you have to keep in mind where you are in the alternating sequence of words and numbers while also fighting the tendency to complete the sequence you have just left. That is, if you say the word 'little' you automatically want to say 'lamb' next, rather than 'four'. Much of the switching cost results from what's known as the 'inhibition of return' – the mental focus needed to stop the mind from sliding backwards into the previous task. Inhibiting one task and starting another – many times in succession – for hour after hour – consumes time and mental energy. Such multi-tasking might feel like you are doing many things at once in parallel, whereas in reality you are simply jumping from one task to another very inefficiently. And the more complex the task, the more inefficient the switching becomes. According to some studies,[1] it can take around twenty minutes to refocus on a complex task after an interruption – and sometimes far longer. Repeated switching has a more insidious consequence, too. As each day progresses, and the weeks move into years, your mind can become shallower and shallower. It begins to erode your attention span. Your mind starts behaving like a skipping stone, bouncing off the surface of a pond. You may become better at switching, but less efficient at focusing on the tasks that you switch to. And because you can hold less and less in your mind, you need to switch more often, which means that you slow down even more as all the different priorities compete for the diminishing space of your mind.

There's an emotional cost too. Because you are focusing your finite mental energy on the difficult task of switching, rather than working, such interruptions make you feel irritable and short-tempered. It can feel like you actually need that little burst of angry energy to switch back to the task that was interrupted. And it's stressful. These changes can become hard-wired into your brain, so that you end up being quicker to anger and slower to laugh.

Nor are these problems confined solely to work. Looking after family and keeping a home running smoothly were once considered major tasks in themselves. Now, often out of necessity, they have been squeezed to the margins. This, in turn, means that maintaining a social life is far more difficult and having some genuine free time can seem all but impossible. Even if you do manage to find a little time for yourself, it might be interrupted by the arrival of an email from your boss, an alert from your calendar or perhaps a ping from a social media or auction site. Even something as simple as picking up the phone to check the time can mean being confronted with a long list of alerts, banners and notifications. Each one grabs a moment of your life – then trying to ignore or suppress them snatches away the next.

None of these is a difficulty in itself, but they can all combine to become a major problem when you have too much to do and not enough time to do it all. In this way, they can add to feelings of being swamped and overwhelmed. And it's hardly surprising, then, that you can end up feeling increasingly frazzled and on the edge of burning out.[2]

Although such a state is distressing and exhausting, something extra is needed to turn it into clinical-level anxiety, stress or depression. It's called *entanglement*; it's when you become so trapped and enmeshed in difficulty that you cannot see a way out, no matter how hard you try. It's when you begin to overthink and to brood; becoming wrapped up in negativity. But it's not the 'negative' feelings themselves that are the problem – they are symptoms; rather, it's the way that they become entangled with each other to deepen and prolong your suffering that is the root of your difficulties. Each one nestles in and supports the others. They can become so intertwined that one sad thought triggers the next, and the next and the next in a vicious downward spiral, dragging down with them your feelings, your body's energy levels and your motivation to do the things that might support and nourish you.

The same is true of all distressing thoughts. Anxious thoughts trigger more anxious thoughts. Stress triggers stress. Each spiral of negativity begins to act like a sticky net that flails around, dredging up more uncomfortable feelings and becoming ever more entangled. As you become more and more distracted, short of time and overwhelmed, it can be ever harder to stop working, stop worrying, stop brooding. Entangled states often take the form of negative open-ended questions that rarely have a definitive answer: *What's up with me today? Where did I go wrong? Why do I always make these mistakes? Why can't I get a grip? I should be happy ... why aren't I happy?* These appear to be open-ended questions, but if you listen, you'll hear what they really are. They're the sound of your inner critic: *There's something wrong; you always make mistakes; get a grip; you should be happy.*

The inner critic snipes from the sidelines, demands perfection and orders you to try harder, whatever the cost. It warns you against weakness, worries for your future and reminds you of past failures. It traps and then entangles you inside your own thoughts with no obvious means of escape. Such negative states can build up so much momentum that they can become extremely difficult to stop. They can lead to increasing agitation as your mind flails around and spirals out of control. Or you might become outwardly angry and aggressive, or perhaps get into verbal or even physical fights. If such agitation continues, you can become exhausted by the struggle and start to feel helpless before quietly slipping into despair and maybe even depression.

Feelings of anxiety, stress, unhappiness and exhaustion can become so entangled that they form a spiky knot of pain at the core of your being. Such entanglement is driven by a fundamental feature of the mind and involves both feeling tones and reactivity pulses. New research shows how it happens – but more importantly, it points to a way out.[3] It's complicated, so an analogy might help:

Think back to the dog in the park running around in tight circles. You may have thought: *Why doesn't she notice the space?* Even though it was all around her, she simply could not see it. She was locked into a pattern of behaviour born out of her sense of being trapped – and this perception was so all-encompassing that she simply could not see her way out, even though she was doing her best and her escape route was right in front of her eyes. The same can happen to us. We can become so entangled with our daily lives that we cannot chart a path to freedom.

Even low-level mental distress can become so all-consuming that we simply cannot escape, no matter how hard we try. Painful though it is, such entanglement is part of the mind's attempt to find freedom from suffering. When your inner critic attacks you, it is, in fact, doing its best to help. But it often tragically back-fires. This happens because of a curious feature of our minds when we rush about, overwork and become overwhelmed.

To understand what is at the root of this entanglement we need to turn to new findings within psychology and neuro-science. Although the details are still being worked out, it is clear that the way we perceive and make sense of the world is dramatically different to what was believed – and this has profound implications for our understanding of the origins of our thoughts, feelings and emotions (and also for many mental-health problems). When these new ideas are incorporated into the practice of mindfulness, they greatly enhance its benefits. They can, however, be a little tricky to understand because they are so wildly counterintuitive, so please bear with us while we explain. After this, it will all make perfect sense, and much of your life's distress will start to evaporate as you put the principles into practice.

THE NEW PSYCHOLOGY OF THE MIND: PREDICTIVE PROCESSING

It takes an enormous amount of mental energy to become con-scious of the present moment. This is because of the vast amount of information flowing in from our senses, all of it needing to be co-ordinated and integrated so that we can become not only conscious of the world but also make decisions and act upon them – in real time – in the *present moment*. Given the complexity of the task, you would expect this to make everything – from walking along a crowded street to avoiding road accidents or even something as simple as catching a ball – extremely difficult. But nature has got around the problem by giving us a brain that predicts the future. It constructs a 'simplified' model of the world that is constantly updated and enriched by information from our senses. What we regard as the present moment is actually a stunningly realistic illusion created by the mind. An illusion so compelling that we mistake it for reality. It is called a *simulation* and the process it relies upon is known as 'predictive processing'.[4] Predictive processing works by constantly 'guessing' what information the senses are about to send to the brain. We do not truly see the world; we see what our minds think the world is about to look like. Nor do we truly hear, but instead experience the sounds that the mind believes are about to hit our ears. And the same is true for our other senses, too. The mind predicts what we are about to taste, feel and smell. And in practice, it is this prediction – or simulation – that we experience, rather than the 'real' world.

As you can imagine, this is a fantastically complex process, but a simple analogy helps here: if you are talking about politics in the UK and someone mentions the Houses of P ... you can guess what's coming next (the word 'Parliament'). Because you have *predicted* the word, you don't need to *listen* to the word itself. You can instead use that moment to capture the meaning of the whole sentence. Such predictions make perception and responses more fluent because the world is normally predictable. As explained above, we don't create a prediction for one single sense but for all of them. Simultaneously. We construct a global model that incorporates sights, sounds, smells, tastes and sensations. This model is constantly updated, moment by moment, and incorporates any deviations from the real external 'reality'; we move through the world creating and updating – predicting and checking – it. And if our checks show that we have made an error (like when we approach a shop door and pull on the large handle rather than pushing on it), we simply begin to pay more attention to the *actual* stream of data arriving from our senses. Any necessary corrections are then built into the model. The mind runs many different variations of the model simultaneously, and each is continuously checked against reality to notice the beginnings of any divergence. The most accurate one 'wins' and becomes a moment in the simulation that we experience.

Each moment in the simulation builds upon the last, as it rolls forwards through time. With each iteration of the model, all incoming data from the senses is compared to the current most accurate model, along with countless variants of it. And then, once again, the most accurate model 'wins' and serves as the foundation for the next iteration. Each model, therefore, spawns others, with each one fanning outwards into the future, slowly diverging from the others. In practice, most of the information flowing through the mind is a kind of 'self-talk' – internally generated predictions that are topped up with data from our senses, the most accurate of which then become incorporated into the simulation.

Even vision is a simulation

There are several major parts of the brain that deal with vision, known as V1 to V6. They shuttle information back and forth between themselves to create the experience of seeing. VI is called the primary visual cortex because it is the first port of call for information from the eye. You would expect that most information that flows into VI to come from the eye alone. After all, it is the eye that does the seeing. But this is not the case. More information flows from other areas of the brain into VI. By some measures, the brain is sending ten times as much information to this part of the visual cortex as the eyes.[5] So, when you close your eyes and imagine an object (say, an orange) or picture a scene such as your first kiss, your brain is sending information to the VI so you can 'see' it. Your mind's eye is using the visual brain to create images. This 'top-down' data flowing into the visual centre of the brain is also used to predict what you are about to see and this is then checked against information from the eyes; so this, too, is the simulation of vision rather than the eye's 'cinematic' vision itself. Rather than passively looking at the world, therefore, you are actually building a world that is then checked against reality moment by moment.

But it's not just vision that works this way. All senses do. And it doesn't end there. It is all combined with information about the state of your body along with your thoughts, feelings and emotions to create your overall state of mind. And all of these fluctuate moment by moment; rising and falling, like waves on the sea.

Such internal models aren't just fast; they are thrifty, too. They radically reduce the effort needed to make sense of the world and grant us the mental space to think and make creative choices. The

brain does this by noticing only the differences between what your senses are receiving and what you were expecting them to receive. This slashes the amount of information needed to be held in the mind and processed. Another analogy might help here: streaming services such as YouTube and Netflix manage to serve up ultra-high-definition video while still being fast and thrifty because they are extremely efficient at compressing movie data. And they do it in ways that are conceptually similar to the way the mind creates its simulation. In the past, broadcasters sent all the data needed to build up a single frame of a film and they did so fifty to sixty times every second. This meant they could only broadcast relatively low-resolution pictures with a limited range of colours and sounds. Streaming services take the opposite approach. They send only the differences between successive movie frames. They can do this because the differences are often only small. Think of a film scene with a red open-topped sports car cruising along a desert highway. The only thing that changes from one frame to the next is the relatively small movement of the car along the road. The shape and colour of the car are almost identical, the sky stays largely the same, as does the desert scenery. Core elements of the film might also be stored in a 'cache' ready for re-use later on (a cache is a specialised area of very fast memory that stores frequently accessed information). So, in practice, for the same bandwidth, a streaming service can send a far more life-like, ultra-high-definition film that contains millions of colours and 3D surround sound.

It turns out, the brain does something similar with sensory information, along with the most commonly experienced thoughts, feelings, emotions and concepts. It has a cache that stores your core experiences ready for re-use in your simulation. Imagine you are walking through your local park on a lovely sunny day. You have been to the park countless times before, and know it in detail. You have seen the sun filtering through the leaves of the trees many times; you know how the grass looks and smells, the sounds made by the children on the swings, the dogs barking and the traffic in the distance. You know how the ground feels under your feet, the sensations the sunlight makes on your skin and how fresh the air feels each time you breathe. You know everything you need to know about the park in order to reconstruct a highly accurate simulation of it in your mind. And if there are a few gaps – well, the mind is perfectly capable of filling them in and constructing a seamless experience. You do not need to sense it directly to feel as if you are experiencing it. Your mind only needs the information about parks that is stored in your long-term memory. This can simply be loaded into the cache as needed and used in the mind's simulation of reality. And the chances are, it is virtually 100 per cent accurate – certainly accurate enough for you to enjoy your walk.

But the cache isn't just a fast memory that allows you to reconstruct places that you have already visited. The core concepts can be used to simulate new places and experiences, too. In practice, if you visit a new park, you can re-use the information that relates to your local park in the new situation. In this example, you can, in effect, experience your old park when you visit the new one. And the same is true for any new situation. When confronted with something new, a quick glance is often enough to trigger memories in the cache which are then used to prime the simulation and build up a 'fast and messy model'. This is then refined and updated as the senses send the mind new information. In practice, a visit to a new park starts off as a simulation of your local one, but as new information arrives, you begin to notice the differences, and these are then built into your global model.

And it's not just visits to a lovely park that are stored in memory. Distressing thoughts, feelings and emotions are stored, too. This is because the cache tends to store the most salient recent experiences, along with your most potent thoughts, feelings and emotions. And unfortunately for us, the most pressing and salient ones are also the most distressing. This means those most likely to be re-experienced in your simulation are the most negative ones. It is far more probable that you will recall anxious, stressful and unhappy thoughts than positive or even neutral ones. So the thoughts most likely to be uploaded into the cache and then held on a hair-trigger are ones such as: *Why is everything so difficult? I'm exhausted. No one is pulling their weight. Everyone expects me to do everything for them. I'm fed up with being taken for granted.* And the same is true for feelings and emotions and also for verbal and physical reactions and even aggression. Such dark and amorphous emotions as anxiety, stress, anger and unhappiness are held at the front of the queue. And because everything is entangled, even a few negative thoughts can unleash a torrent. These can trigger other powerful negative emotions. And all the while, these emotions are triggering physical changes in the body, too: pains in your neck or shoulder might appear; a headache might start brewing; or perhaps anxious butterflies in your stomach might transform into sickness.

None of this means that your distress is exaggerated or untrue. Nor are you overreacting, being overly sensitive or 'weak' in some way. If you feel sad, then you are sad. If you feel anxious, stressed, exhausted or angry, then you truly are experiencing such distress. Your predictions *are true for you.* Simulation *is* reality.

Painful though they are, these states of distress are also ones of hope. For you will soon come to realise that they are not solid, real and unchanging. And something quite pure and simple lies beneath them. Something that sits between the 'essence' of you and your experience of the world. It fluctuates moment by moment. Moments that are either pleasant, unpleasant or neutral. The feeling tones of the moment. And it is these that guide your subsequent thoughts, feelings, emotions and physical sensations and also your reactions to them. They prime your mind to create a world that is either positive and uplifting, dark and forbidding or something in between.

And once you have made contact with the underlying stream of feeling tones, something remarkable can begin to happen. Simply paying attention to them, warmly greeting them as they rise and fall, is enough for all their tangles to simply unravel of their own accord. Even your darkest thoughts, feelings and emotions will begin to dissolve. Your mind begins to clear, leaving you free to directly experience the world in all its sensory joy.

Feeling tones of the *Doing* and *Being* states of mind and body

In our previous book, *Mindfulness: Finding Peace in a Frantic World*, we explained that many of our difficulties result from trying to logically solve emotional problems. This is because when you try to solve an emotional difficulty, you deploy one of the mind's most powerful tools: rational, critical thinking. This is done using the mind's *Doing* mode – its rational and logical way of approaching the world and of thinking and solving problems. It's one of the most useful and powerful devices in our mental toolbox. It excels at solving problems, such as juggling work schedules, navigating across a city, organising logistics chains and generally getting things done. The Doing mode works by progressively narrowing the gap between where you are and where you want to be. It does so by subconsciously breaking down the problem into pieces, each of which is solved in the mind's eye (mental models again), and the solution is then re-analysed to see whether it's got you any closer to your goal.

But when it comes to emotions, this approach can backfire because it requires you to focus on the gap between how you feel now (unhappy) and how you'd like to feel (happy). Focusing on the gap highlights it, bringing it into sharp relief, magnifying it and making it all-consuming. In this way, an emotional difficulty is converted into a logical problem that demands to be solved. And in so doing, you ask yourself such tough, critical questions as: *Why can't I get a grip on this? What's wrong with me? Where did I go wrong? Why do I always make these mistakes?* Such questions are not only harsh and self-destructive, but also demand that the mind furnishes the evidence to explain its discontent. Very quickly, your mind can produce a list of reasons why you can't get a grip, why you continuously make mistakes and where you have gone wrong in life. These are then built into your mental models.

Using the Doing mode in this way is disastrous because emotions are not 'solid' and unchanging, so they cannot be 'solved' in any logical and concrete way. They are not problems to be solved but messages to be felt. Once the message has been delivered (that is, felt), it has done its job, so it will tend to evaporate like the mist on a spring morning. And this holds true for all our most troubling feelings and emotions, whether they be anxiety, stress, unhappiness, anger or exhaustion. Although there is nothing inherently wrong with the Doing mode, it can become a problem when it runs amok and volunteers for a job that it simply cannot do, such as solving an emotional problem. For this reason, when it starts to chase its own tail, it morphs into the *Driven-Doing* mode (we call it the Driven mode). This is when you become bogged down inside your thoughts. Inside your simulation. It is when your mind's cache and predictive processor become so tightly coupled that all you can experience are the same things over and over again – the same thoughts, feelings and emotions. Driven mode is a symptom of a suffering mind.

Signs of the Driven mode

Driven mode has seven main characteristics that indicate when it has taken over the mind:

- **Distracted** You find it harder to keep your mind on one thing; your attention is easily pushed and pulled by things around you, or by your own thoughts, memories or daydreams.
- **Judgmental** You get into a battle with your mind, becoming judgmental and unkind towards yourself, and less tolerant of others, too.

- **Emotional** You rush through life and don't see the tipping points for your emotions. You may find yourself having an emotional meltdown without warning.
- **Off balance** You find yourself at the mercy of your moods. When you try to resist the negative, it escalates and becomes even worse; when you try to get more of the positives, they slip through your fingers, so you learn to ignore or dismiss them to avoid future disappointment.
- **Reactive** Your mind constantly gears up for action that may never be taken, and you become exhausted as your body's energy is used up by imagined plans and strategies.
- **Avoidant** You find yourself suppressing, avoiding or trying to escape from even the smallest of difficulties because the mood feels intolerable.
- **Joyless** To focus on your preoccupations, the mind damps down everything else, even your positive states of mind, such as happiness and joy. You then find it increasingly difficult to get things done or to find fulfilment in life.

You cannot stop the triggering of negative thoughts, feelings and emotions, but you can stop what happens next. You can stop the vicious cycle from feeding off itself and triggering wave after wave of negativity. You can do this by harnessing an alternative way of relating to yourself and the world. The mind can do so much more than logically crunch through problems. You can also become *aware* that you are thinking. You can connect directly with the world using your senses. You can experience it without your mental cache acting as a distorting filter. Such pure awareness is known as the *Being* mode.

Being mode allows you to step outside of the mind's natural tendency to over-think, overanalyse and overjudge. Throughout the ages, people have learned how to cultivate this Being mode through meditation. And this course takes the process further by going 'upstream', into the moment you become aware of your thinking, feeling and sensing. Moments of vedana. Moments of clarity that will, ultimately, set you free.

Although a driven state of mind can be distressing, its seven characteristics can also be used as entry points into the realm of feeling tones. And it is these entry points that are explored and harnessed in the practice chapters of *Deeper Mindfulness*.

CHAPTER THREE

Frame by Frame

The year was 1877 and the photographer was the Englishman Eadweard Muybridge.[1] The dispute, which had raged for centuries, was whether there was any moment in the gallop of a horse when all four hooves were off the ground simultaneously. To settle the argument, it took twelve cameras carefully positioned along a horse track in Palo Alto, California, with a thread strung across the circuit from each camera. As the horse ran past, it broke the threads and released each camera's shutter. When the photographs were developed, they revealed the answer. And yes, there was a brief moment when the horse floated above the ground. The use of this new technology of carefully arranged cameras allowed Muybridge to capture a new view, frame by frame, which no one had seen before.

This book invites you to bring a similar approach to the activity of your own mind and body. It requests that you pay attention to what your body senses in the present moment; to what it is *actually* seeing, hearing, touching, tasting and smelling. And as you do so, it asks you to pay attention to what the mind itself is doing. Is it engaged with a task or lost in thinking, remembering, planning, daydreaming or worrying? And what happens immediately *after* any sensation, thought, feeling or emotion first arises? To see all of this, frame by frame, is to discover a new world. A world free of simulation. One glimpsed directly. This isn't just an abstract or esoteric idea. Your quality of life depends upon it. For such momentary insights can give you a valuable early-warning signal of the impulses that can upend your world. It enables you to sense and make allowances for the thoughts, feelings and emotions that trigger your most distressing reactions. It grants you a moment in which you can choose whether to respond rather than react. And, as we saw in earlier chapters, inside each of these moments lies a hidden element. In the world of ancient India, and in the traditions that arose from it, it was known as vedana.[2] We know it as feeling tone, or more simply, the 'feel' of an experience.

Feeling tone is that first sense of whether anything is pleasant, unpleasant or neutral. It is not a feeling in the sense of an emotion – a deep sadness or high excitement, agitated worry or unhurried relaxation – but a much simpler sense of the pleasantness or unpleasantness of an experience. It is an instant, automatic, wordless 'felt sense'. You just *know* it when it appears. You don't have to consciously judge it or think about it. It has a simple purity.

Yet, feeling tones can be unpredictable. You can never know in advance the flavour of their appearance. They don't exist in objects themselves but instead emerge from their contact with your mind and body in *combination* with the state of your body and mind at that precise moment. As an example, you might normally find chocolate cake pleasant, but if you have just eaten a heavy meal, the very thought of it might feel unpleasant. Or if you are busy, the ping of an arriving message might feel like an unpleasant distraction, but if you are feeling lonely, the same sound might create a pleasant feeling tone. This ever-changing landscape of contexts and moods makes it difficult to predict what will strike you as pleasant or unpleasant. The only certain way of knowing is to pay attention in the *now*. And because feeling tones often arise and pass away quickly, they can be difficult to notice, unless you intentionally cultivate awareness of them. Noticing them, however, is critically important because they shape what happens next. *Pleasant* feeling tones tend to trigger a desire for more moments that are similar. *Unpleasant* feeling tones tend to trigger a sense of 'aversion', of pushing away, of resistance. *Neutral* ones encourage you to 'tune out' – for example, you may find yourself getting a little bored, perhaps hoping this chapter could hurry up and move on to the next thing. Such reactivity pulses, as they are known, are so compelling – and arise so fast – that they can sweep you along in a current of thoughts before you even notice their presence. Without being aware of it, an unpleasant moment may tip you into a negative direction that can last for hours, days or even beyond. A pleasant moment may arrive, but in your hunger for it to last a little longer, you may try to grasp hold of it, only to discover it slipping through your fingers. This triggers waves of frustration and feelings of loss. Existential angst, even. In such ways, feeling tones can be tipping points for the quality of the next moment.

Although you cannot change or control feeling tones, you can control what happens next. Mindful awareness can become a checkpoint that allows you to intercept any waves of reactivity or emotional distress before they spiral out of control. It stops such reactivity pulses from dominating your life with all the distress they bring. As meditation teacher Joseph Goldstein says: 'Mindfulness of feeling tone is one of the master keys that both reveals and unlocks the deepest patterns of our conditioning.'[3]

This is hidden knowledge – part of the wisdom tradition that has influenced the practice of meditation for millennia – but is only ever rarely made explicit. And its true significance has only recently come to the fore. Neuroscience has now discovered the importance of this 'first impression': it is fundamental to all life. Just as plants arch towards sunlight, and roots stretch towards water, so every living being has the means to discern the pleasant from the unpleasant. *All life depends upon it.*

Feeling tones are immediate and rely on sensitivities built into every cell of our bodies from the earliest days of our evolution. Even single-celled creatures are sensitive to both nutrients and toxins. It allows them to distinguish between one and the other.[4] This is the essence of vedana. It helps all living beings distinguish between the things that they should move towards (pleasant) and those that they should move away from (unpleasant) and encourages them to sit tight if everything is fine (neutral). Without such a sensitivity, they would be like a boat without a rudder, with nothing to steer them away from danger and towards a friendly port.

In countless ways, vedana marks the difference between life and mere machinery.

But we humans have a unique and special difficulty when it comes to vedana: our mental life is so complex that we can become lost inside of it. Our thoughts, memories and plans, which also carry feeling tones, can compel us to flee from our own minds. *And while we can flee, we can never escape.*

This was Alice's predicament. She had spent many years mired in mental and physical pain – truly inescapable pain that she could trace back to a moment in time many years earlier.

In her teens, Alice was a promising athlete. She was especially good at the high jump – a skill that had unfortunate consequences for her as an adult when she developed chronic back pain. She was convinced she knew what it was and was eventually referred to a specialist. She explained to the physician that it was the result of a high-jump accident she'd had as a teenager.

'My mother was against me doing the sport because she thought it was dangerous,' she said. 'So I had to sneak away to do competitions. But I'm a rebellious spirit, always have been, and the county championships were coming up, so what could I do other than secretly take part? And I won! So of course, my mother found out anyway.

'In those days we only had sand to land in and my winning jump left me quite badly hurt. I landed awkwardly and hurt the coccyx in my back. My back has given me trouble ever since. The worst part of the whole episode wasn't so much the pain; it was my mother telling me off for having the accident. Even now, I can still hear her shouting at me: "You only have yourself to blame! It's all your own stupid fault! Look at you – you could have ruined your life!" So whenever my back hurt, I could hear my mother's voice telling me off for injuring myself. And she was right. It *was* my fault. I went against what she said and paid the price.'

When the consultant analysed the scans, she discovered that Alice's coccyx was perfectly healthy. The pain had nothing to do with her accident at all. What's more, she said: 'You've been too hard on yourself, which is making you feel even worse. The way that you've been punishing yourself emotionally has amplified your pain.'

Although Alice's story is quite dramatic, it serves to illustrate a wider point: both physical and mental suffering can be made far worse by the stories we tell ourselves, occasionally leading us to completely misunderstand the true cause of our distress. We may think that our suffering is caused by one thing (a damaged coccyx in Alice's case), but it might be the result of something else entirely. This strange state of affairs happens because of the way that we use stories to make sense of our experiences – to understand them, giving them a meaning that we can then build into our mental model to help us survive and prosper in a complex world. In many ways, we are story machines. Give any one of us a scrap or two of information and, within moments, we will have woven it into a gripping yarn – a comedy or tragedy as powerful as any Shakespearean drama. This would not be so bad if we spent our time creating positive and uplifting stories, but usually we don't. In fact, we often end up doing the opposite because the most salient information, the information stored in our mental cache, tends to be 'negative'. And as every Hollywood director will tell you, the most compelling stories focus on pain, struggle, fear, horror, tragedy and loss. But often, it is not the stories themselves that do the 'damage' to our wellbeing but, rather, our reactions to them. Our minds tend to overreact both to events and the stories they inspire. Like Alice, we can end up angrily criticising ourselves and others for things that have gone wrong. Such negative thoughts can spark a cascade of other equally troubling ones, with our minds obsessively going around the same track, alternating between angry self-justification and painful self-blame. One thought triggers the next, and the next and the next, so that very quickly, we find ourselves mired in anger, worry, stress, unhappiness and, ultimately, exhaustion. These are all signs that the Driven mode has hijacked the mind (see pages 25–9).

In this way, echoes from the past can have powerful repercussions in the present, going on to lay the groundwork for troubles to come. And unless we are mindful, a genuine accident can lead us to relentlessly punish ourselves for having made such a 'mistake'; 'failure' at school can embed fear, anxiety and stress; and rebukes from parents can create a world of psychological pain.

The effect of all this on Alice's pain was evident to the physician but not to her. And although the physical pain was unpleasant enough, it also dredged up powerful thoughts and feelings linked to it: guilt and shame, for sure, but also anger at herself and her mother. Each of these thoughts and feelings arrived with its own unpleasant feeling tone that then became entwined with her existing pain to make it even more unpleasant. As the feeling tones cascaded into the following moments, Alice began to feel ever more trapped. All she could imagine was a future dominated by nothing but pain and suffering.

But there remained a sliver of hope. Although Alice's pain was dragging up all her past hurt, and this was making things far worse for her, it was, in fact, the feeling tones in the *present* moment that were maintaining her suffering. This is so important that it needs to be emphasised: it is not your past that creates your troubles; it is what is going on *right now* that does so. The only power a memory holds over you is its power to influence your feeling tones – and your subsequent reactions to them – in the *present moment*. This has huge implications. Although feeling tones arise moment by moment and cannot be changed, your reactions in the very next moments *are* potentially flexible. Suffering does not have to cascade into the future. Alternative futures are available to you.

An analogy might help. Think back to your school days. Remember the experiment where iron filings were sprinkled on to a piece of paper while a magnet was moved around underneath? The iron filings danced as if they were alive. The patterns they made were quite entrancing. And what happened when you took the magnet away? The filings collapsed in a lifeless heap. Vedana is like that hidden magnet, with a force field making the mind dance to its tune, just like those iron filings. Because the feelings it generates are so compelling, we cannot quite bring ourselves to take our eyes off the story being played out above the surface. We don't see the forces that are creating the story and keeping it alive. The unpleasantness we feel is therefore not a distressing side effect of our painful thoughts and memories; it is actually bringing them to life. It's the master of ceremonies. We are going to say more about this crucial discovery in later chapters, but for now, it is enough to know that these ever-shifting feeling tones are natural and automatic. You cannot control them. *But you can control what happens next.*

Letting go of the past

Evolution has pre-programmed you to not like unpleasant feeling tones, so it produces resistance – the urge to move away from it. This generates more unpleasantness. And it is this spiral that feeds back into the story and maintains the rumination.

You may have been told to 'let go of the past' many times by friends, family and even therapists, but not how to do it. Understanding the hidden power of feeling tone is the key to doing so. And this is what you will learn to do over the coming weeks.

Cast your mind back to Chapter Two and the discoveries about the mind's predictive-processing model of the world. It has become apparent that when an unpleasant feeling tone arises and triggers a wave of distress, this can cascade forwards into the next moment because of the way that the brain caches this 'peak pain' and readies it for re-use in the following moments. This means that your experience of the next moment is driven by the cache – so you're stuck in a virtual 'video loop', featuring the most intense distress of the past few moments. Such unpleasant-ness moves forwards like a wave, with successive images keeping alive the peak pain and distress. But it can be even worse than this – because it also triggers waves of aversion and a corres-ponding need to escape.[5] These are unpleasant, which furthers your distress. And when the underlying distress does eventually dissipate, your mental model doesn't realise that anything has changed; that the need to escape has passed. Unless the *current* feelings or sensations are strong or precise enough to override the echoes of the last few moments, your experience will continue to be based on the mental models and not the actual data.

This is where mindfulness comes in. It works by gently refreshing the mind's cache. This allows you to see the world as it *is*, not as you *expect* it to be, or *fear* it might become. It is then that something quite remarkable begins to happen. You start to sense the underlying feeling tones that guide all your subsequent thoughts, feelings and emotions, and shape everything that you see, hear, feel, taste and smell. So there arises a sense of having more choice. Of being less in the grip of a mood. You are less likely to reach for the 'relief' of external supports and distrac-tions, such as snacks, alcohol or the need to check your phone.

So much of life is a reaction to what happened in the previous moment. Every feeling tone, also stored in the mind's cache, affects the mental models that you are building. These simulate the world, moment by moment. These are what you experience as the 'real' world. And they lie at the root of so much of life's discontent. But it's not even the feeling tones and your reaction to them that are the problem but ignorance of their existence and of their underlying nature. All you are aware of is the deluge of thoughts, feelings and emotions that follows in their wake. The feeling tones themselves simply pass you by unnoticed.

Sensing your feeling tones gives you a way out. It helps you to make allowances for your entirely natural biases; to compassionately accept that although you might be anxious, stressed, angry or depressed in *this* moment, it is possible to change course for a better life. Then you progressively learn how to let go of your most troubling states of mind. When you do so, something quite magical starts to happen: a sense of peace and joy begins to reappear in your life. You become your own master of ceremonies.

Where do feeling tones come from?

Feeling tones arise in large part from a process known as interoception.[6] This can be seen as a 'dashboard', or internal sense, that keeps track of what's going on inside the body from moment to moment. Interoception helps the body to monitor its internal environment as it maintains such things as energy levels, hormone balances and pH, salt and mineral concentrations.[7] Although scientists are still working out the details, it is clear that the body fuses all this information together into such generalised feelings as hunger and thirst and such broad impulses as a desire to move towards something or away from it. These interoceptive feelings then feed into the mind's mental models and, ultimately, affect its simulation of the world. The process is fantastically complex and dominated by subtle feedback loops, with information from mental models and simulations feeding back into the interoceptive network, which then affects how the body prepares to react.

Interoception is central to life, even if we are barely aware of it. Firstly, we need it to stay alive because it is intimately involved with maintaining the body's internal environment. Secondly, it helps the body manage and budget its resources. For example, if you are going for a run, it will help prepare your body by dilating blood vessels, increasing heart rate and readying energy supplies. But the interoceptive network also has an intimate knowledge of your body's current resources because it keeps an inventory. This means it can budget them and decide how much effort it can afford to dedicate to each activity. In fact, it prepares for action – constantly – just in case these resources are needed. In practice, your body prepares for action in tandem with your mental models and their resulting simulations. This means that as far as your interoceptive network is concerned, your mental landscape – whether regrets about the past or hopes or worries for the future – is treated as if it were absolutely real, right now, and it reacts accordingly (see Chapter Nine for more details). Mind and body constantly prepare for action – if only fleetingly – as one scenario is superseded by another and then another, and preparations to act sweep constantly through them. We are reactivity embodied.

As the internal 'weather pattern' of your body and mind changes from moment to moment, the vedana of the moment changes, too. For example, when you are anxious or stressed, the unpleasant feel of the mental scenarios creates a sense of avoidance or resistance. Such constant vigilance is exhausting because your body prepares for action over and over again. The interoceptive network then senses that your resources are becoming depleted and should be conserved. Anything outside of your immediate concern is pushed away, devalued. If it happens too often, then even the feeling tones of the things that you used to love become unpleasant. This can lead to exhaustion and depression as your motivation evaporates. From there, it can become a vicious downward spiral.

CHAPTER FOUR

Practicalities of
the Programme

The remaining chapters of this book are dedicated to the meditation programme itself. Each of the following eight chapters corresponds to one week of the programme. Each contains two elements: the first is the meditation practice, which usually takes ten to twenty minutes a day; the second is an 'Everyday Mindfulness' practice. The links that will enable you to download or stream all the guided meditations for that particular week can be found in the 'Practices for Week ...' boxes within these chapters.

You also will find detailed instructions for the meditations in the highlighted boxes in each chapter. When you begin the programme, you will probably find it helpful to read through the meditation instructions first, to familiarise yourself with them, before doing the practices using the audio guidance. See if it's possible for you to focus on the spirit of the meditation, rather than becoming hung up on the specifics. Many people read through the whole book before starting the programme. If you do this, we recommend rereading each chapter before you start on the corresponding week of the programme. Each week is built on many centuries of wisdom, backed up by the latest scientific discoveries, so it's preferable for this to be fresh in your mind.

CORE PRACTICES

Each week uses a different guided meditation. Most come in three different lengths: ten, twenty and thirty minutes. This allows you to choose one that suits the time you have available. For example, you may choose to do a ten-minute version in the morning and in the evening or, alternatively, a single twenty-minute version once a day. You should also aim to do the thirty-minute version of each meditation on at least one occasion each week. If you plan on meditating shortly after returning home, you might like to have a small snack or drink first. Even low-level hunger or thirst can be surprisingly distracting, as can an unnoticed need to go to the toilet. If you meditate in the early morning, you may find that you have to get up and go to bed a little earlier, so that the practice isn't carried out at the expense of sleep or in a rush. Regularity is important, too, as it cuts down on procrastination. At first, you might find it difficult to make the time, but meditation tends to liberate more time than it consumes. It is, however, very important that you do make a commitment to yourself to carry out the meditations. They require practice, but don't forget that they have been proven to help many people. They do, however, work best if you put in the required time each day. To embed these benefits, you will need to commit to completing the eight-week course. Remember, too, that they may not appear to have instant benefits. However, many people do report feeling more relaxed and happier almost from day one.

After working with a guided meditation for a day or two, you can then choose how you wish to practise. For example, you may choose to continue using a fully guided meditation or to use the 'minimal instructions' (Mi) version for the rest of that week. As you progress through each week of the course, you may eventually prefer to use the silent track that simply has a timing bell every five minutes. Once familiar with a meditation, you can, of course, do the meditation yourself without any guidance or timer at all. If you do either of the latter two, feel free to go back to one of the fully guided tracks at any time to refresh your memory. Even the most experienced of meditators follow guided meditations from time to time. Note that many people have found that keeping a regular journal or diary of their experiences helps embed the benefits of meditation.

Throughout this course, it is important to realise that you can take a break from your daily practice at any time. Ask yourself from time to time: *Is this what I need right now?* Or, *Is this helping me?* And if you feel that it isn't, feel free to let go of your practice for a while and to return when you feel ready to continue.

EVERYDAY MINDFULNESS

As mentioned above, the second element of the programme is known as 'Everyday Mindfulness'. These are simple practices designed, as you would expect, to embed mindfulness into everyday life. They consist of such things as consciously paying attention to the world around you as you wake up in the morning, or perhaps bringing mindful attention to a drink, meal or snack. As well as embedding mindfulness into your life, these gradually break down the negative habits of thinking and behaving that exert a subtle but powerful hold over you. They will help you to progressively transition into new and more creative ways of thinking. You should aim to carry these out in an inquisitive and playful state of mind.

Try to carry out the meditations on six days out of seven. It does not matter which day you choose to take a break. The Everyday Mindfulness tasks should be performed as the instructions in each chapter suggest. Don't worry if you miss a day or two of meditation. Simply make up the time on the other days. When you have done so, you can then carry on with the next week of the programme. If you only manage to meditate on three days or fewer, then it's recommended that you repeat that week. These meditations gain their power through repetition, so it is important that you do your best to meditate on the recommended number of days. Life, however, can be busy, so it's not unusual to pause or stop for a while. If you should stop meditating completely for more than a few weeks, you should restart the programme. And if this happens, see if it is possible to do this without criticising yourself.

It's surprisingly common to make several 'false' starts or to take breaks when you start on any meditation programme. Instead of being tough on yourself, gently remind yourself that *you cannot fail at mindfulness*. We mean that; you can't. The programme may, however, take longer to complete than you might wish. If this is the case, simply pick up the reins when you feel able. Making repeated false starts – or taking a long time to find a natural place for meditation in your life – can be important lessons in their own right. If you feel that you are not making as much 'progress' as you might wish (or that you are not trying hard enough), then, once again, try to avoid criticising yourself. Learning to treat yourself with compassion and gaining an understanding of your own life are important elements of the programme. In their own ways, they also bolster courage and resilience.

The core programme takes eight weeks. You may find that you want to continue meditating when the formal programme has finished. To help you with this, the final chapter of the book shows you how to build awareness of feeling tone into your life for the long term.

Week-by-week summary of the programme

The aim of this book is to help you deepen your mindfulness practice by exploring the feeling tone that accompanies every moment of awareness. Although it is an important underlying theme in all mindfulness practices and courses, it is largely implicit and hidden. This programme brings it out into the open.

The first two weeks act as foundation stones for the whole course. If you are new to mindfulness, they will teach you the core skills necessary to progress through the programme. If you have meditation experience, they will begin to teach you the subtly different skills needed for the later feeling tone practices. Although these skills may seem familiar, you will still gain a lot from practising them, as they emphasise differing aspects of mindfulness and, inch by inch, reveal how your feeling tones guide your thoughts, feelings, emotions and behaviour.

- **Week One** You will begin to explore different ways of 'anchoring' your attention in the present moment. This is the place to which you'll bring your attention when the mind inevitably wanders. In traditional mindfulness, the breath often acts as the anchor. Following the sensations of breathing, and how they change from moment to moment, is one of the central skills of mindfulness. But some people find focusing on the breath to be an uncertain anchor, so we instead invite you to explore such alternatives as paying attention to moment-to-moment changes in the physical sensations in your feet or hands, or your contact with what you are sitting or lying on.

- **Week Two** You'll begin exploring how to relate differently towards mind-wandering. Many people, particularly if they have practised mindfulness for some time, find that when their minds wander, they tend to rush back to the breath, almost as if they have been discovered doing something wrong. But realising that the mind has wandered is exactly what you need to do. The moment you realise that your mind has wandered is a moment of mindfulness. So in Week Two we ask you to build on this moment by deliberately pausing for a short while and then bringing a sense of gratitude to your mind for all the hard work it is doing for you, including noticing the loss of focus. Such positive reinforcement not only enhances wellbeing but is also more effective in the long run.

Having laid these foundations, you will then be asked to explore your feeling tones in three consecutive stages over the ensuing three weeks: firstly, whenever the mind wanders; secondly, while doing mindful walking; and thirdly, during each out-breath. Taken together, these three weeks progressively build the core skills of feeling-tone awareness – the skills that will transform your life. These weeks will teach you to recognise the elusive and ever-changing nature of tonality and how much of what you think, feel and do depends as much on your underlying feeling tones as on conscious rational thinking. Once you have learned this in a real and visceral way, you will be in a position to regain control over your life once again.

- **Week Three** The meditation for Week Three begins this process by asking you to focus on the feeling tone in the moment that you become aware of bodily sensations and when your mind begins to wander (or, at least when you first realise it has wandered). Through this, you will come to realise that distractions are often minor in themselves, but the mind tends to whip them up into a storm and create a sense of urgency. It is this sense of urgency that often undermines quality of life. During Week Three you will begin to see this process in action. You will come to learn that the mind craves to hold on to the pleasant, push away the unpleasant and tune out the neutral. This is the origin of so much of our suffering. We can tell you this – we can even prove it to you with the most powerful tools available to science – but it is only when you actually feel it in your bones that you will finally come to believe it.
- **Week Four** Here, you will begin to use what you have learned in the course to help you stop your mind from

entering the spirals of craving that destroy quality of life. Simply tuning in to, observing and then allowing the feeling tone to remain just as it is, is one of the most powerful techniques you will ever learn for settling the mind and enhancing quality of life. Day by day in Week Four, you will progressively begin to accept your feeling tones as they arise and fade away again: you will learn to respond to pleasant feeling tones by first recognising them as pleasant and then gently saying to yourself, 'It's OK to like this'; you will learn to respond to unpleasant feeling tones by first recognising them as unpleasant and then saying to yourself, 'It's OK not to like this.' This simple act will allow you to watch those noisy and insistent voices of guilt, craving and suffering simply evaporate.

- **Week Five** This will further extend your practice by helping you to notice in forensic detail the way that feeling tones often appear to have lives of their own. They fluctuate moment by moment. The meditations this week enhance your perspective by allowing you to see more clearly those aspects of life that pass you by simply because your mind is too busy being reactive – gearing up for action which is not necessary and which, in any case, will not be carried out. Such busyness ensures that all too often, you simply do not see or appreciate the small things in your life. These 'small' things often aren't so small. They are the foundations on which a happy and meaningful life are built. To this end, Week Five will help you to recognise when the mind is getting over-busy and restless, and instead allow you to turn towards the small, pleasant things that exist in even the most challenging and difficult of times. And when difficulties do arise, such perspective forestalls the mind's tendency to create anxiety, stress and unhappiness out of endless imaginary scenarios based on 'if onlys' and 'what ifs'.

During Weeks Three, Four and Five, other practices are also introduced that will help embed what you have learned through meditation. These 'Everyday Mindfulness' practices include such things as an 'appreciation practice' where you are asked to remember some of the little things that make life quite magical and an end-of-day reflection on the overall feeling tone of your day and the main themes that ran through it.

- **Week Six** Here, you extend this important wisdom into everyday life. You will learn how to cope with the things that regularly bother you but whose effects are often hard to see because they are hidden – masquerading as something else, yet chipping away at your mood and quality of life, leaving you exhausted.
- **Week Seven** This is where you'll learn about procrastination and how to take action to do more of the things that enhance quality of life and to work more skilfully with the things that diminish it.
- **Week Eight** You will learn in Week Eight how to draw up a plan to sustain your discoveries and to further enhance your practices.

A TIME AND A PLACE FOR MEDITATION

There will be many times when you feel you do not have any spare time to meditate. This is undoubtedly true. Life is busy and you have many priorities to juggle. So if you did have any spare time, the chances are you would already have allocated it to something else by now. You do have to *make* time to meditate, but in the long run you will earn that time back since maintaining a meditation practice helps to streamline life. If you are still concerned by this commitment, gently ask yourself how much time you spend each day worrying, procrastinating and running through seemingly pointless habits. Maybe you could promise yourself to devote part of this time to meditation?

Some people are put off starting a meditation programme because they fear it might be seen as 'self-indulgent'. If this concerns you, perhaps you could see it as a fitness programme for the mind. Many people spend several hours a week running or working out at the gym. Why not spend a little time each day doing the same thing for your mind?

Where ...

It is best to meditate in a pleasant and peaceful place. This can be as simple as a tranquil corner of your home. Try to avoid the bedroom because this might encourage drowsiness. However, if this is the quietest and most tranquil space available to you, it's OK to meditate there. You might also like to let others in your home know that you would like to remain undisturbed while you practise. Some people find this a little embarrassing, fearing that others will think mindfulness a little odd. In practice, your friends and family will probably be pleased that you are finding the time to enhance your life.

And what equipment will you need? You will need only a phone or computer to listen to the meditation tracks (or to stream them to a TV, headset or hi-fi), a chair to sit on and perhaps a blanket to keep your legs warm. If you use your phone to listen to the meditations, it will be helpful to turn off notifications, switch it to silent or divert calls to voicemail. Each week's meditation tracks can be found by following the QR code or web address shown in each chapter's practices for the week box.

... how

Most people find that sitting on a straight-backed chair is good for meditation, but it's also fine to use a meditation cushion or bench to sit on. If sitting feels difficult, then the meditations can be done lying down on a rug or mat.

If sitting, see if it's possible to adopt an alert posture, upright but not stiff, with your spine self-supporting, about 2–3cm from the back of the chair. It often helps the posture to sit a little towards the front of the chair and to put a small cushion on the seat, so that your hips are slightly higher than your knees. This will allow your back to follow its natural curves and create a sense of openness in the chest. It will also encourage alertness and emotional 'brightness'. The feet should be flat on the floor, about hip-width apart. This encourages a feeling of strength and stability. The hands are best left relaxed, supported by the lap or the thighs.

The best position is one that causes as little muscular strain as possible, while encouraging an alert but relaxed state of mind. Whatever position you choose, remember that you will gain nothing by forcing yourself into a harsh or uncomfortable one. You certainly shouldn't feel the need to sit cross-legged on the floor. Newspapers and magazines love pictures of people meditating in this posture, but there really is no need to do so. While some people do meditate in this way, it is often extremely uncomfortable if you are not used to it. Sitting crossed-legged has nothing to do with the practice of meditation. It is simply the way people traditionally sat in the East.

You may need to shift positions part-way through a meditation. Again, this is OK. Fidgeting is normal, too, and even experienced meditators need to move from time to time. If you do move, see if you can include this in your meditation, moving with full awareness, sensing how the feeling tone fluctuates before, during and after the movement.

... and when?

Why not close your eyes for a few moments, take a deep breath, and begin right now?

CHAPTER FIVE

Week One: Finding Your Ground

Josy took another gulp of her mojito. It was her third within half an hour. She started moving in time with the music and looked out across the crowded living room of her friend's flat. It was stuffed full of people singing, dancing and waving their brightly coloured drinks in the air. Saturday night was turning into a bit of a riot, which was just the way Josy liked it.

The tall stranger once again wandered over and attempted to strike up a conversation. She'd evaded his advances earlier, but this time she responded with a smile. He leaned a little closer, trying to make himself heard above the sounds of the party. She could just about hear his words, but then a different voice cut through the noise of the room: 'Josy was telling me about that mad hitchhike back from Italy ...' As soon as her name was mentioned, Josy's mind focused on the conversation on the other side of the room. She heard every word, with crystal clarity, as if the room had fallen into silence.

We've all experienced this so-called 'cocktail-party effect', where we are in a noisy place and suddenly find ourselves snapping to attention when someone mentions our name. Sometimes it can be even more powerful than this, such as when you hear the few words before your name is even mentioned. In such moments, it can feel as if time has flowed backwards a few seconds and allowed you to catch up with the world. And in a sense, this is what happens.

The cocktail-party effect arises out of the mind's astonishing ability to gather disparate information from its senses, fuse it all together and analyse its significance. This data is then used to update our different 'models of reality', with the one that best fits crystallising to become our actual experience (see pages 18–25). Often, we only get an inkling of this process when the mind 'jumps the tracks' from one model to another and we experience such things as this cocktail-party effect. It can be powerful and, occasionally, eerie.

Central to this process is the brain's capacity to monitor the world for important information that signals when you might need to update your global model – or switch to an entirely different track. From moment to moment, your brain compares the mind's predictions with the actual incoming data from the senses and looks out for 'surprises' – or prediction errors. If it detects such an error, your attention switches towards the source of the surprise – the voice that has just spoken your name, for example – to see whether the model needs updating. Often, only a little tweaking is needed, but, for an instant, there is an uncertainty that needs to be resolved in case more significant action is needed, and so your attention is inexorably drawn to anything new or surprising. All animals are sensitive to movements in their peripheral vision because it indicates the possible presence of a predator. And humans are no different. Evolution has hard-wired our brains to look out for many such 'distractors', and we don't have a choice whether we notice them or not. Ever found yourself incessantly distracted by a flickering TV above a bar? Put it down to your primate ancestors.

We can also learn to look out for other distractors and these can become written into the mind's 'software'. Hearing your own name in a crowded room is one example, but so too are conversations that resonate with you. Looking to move house, buy a car or take a holiday? Suddenly, you start to notice references to them everywhere and feel compelled to pay attention. Normally, though, after a few moments of heightened awareness, you slip back into your own thoughts and are, perhaps, left in awe of your mind's ability to keep track of the world.

In practice, even if you are focusing on one thing and trying to ignore everything else, your mind continues monitoring the world in the background in case something important needs attending to. Often, though, your attention isn't waylaid in such an obvious fashion but is, instead, subverted without you realising it. Such subversion is often far more insidious and powerful in the long run than any number of cocktail-party hijackings.

It works like this: if you are not paying attention – really paying attention – then you will not notice the accumulating 'prediction errors' that allow you to keep a tight grip on reality. It is these prediction errors that, when *noticed*, keep us in contact with the real world and prevent us from living inside a discon-nected simulation. They provide the exciting little jolts that bring us back into full consciousness and spark our curiosity. They are the source of life's joy. They provide the magic – the stardust – that makes life worth living.

The message is in the error.

Allow us to explain this seemingly irrational idea.

If you are eating your favourite treat, your mind will predict how it tastes and feels in your mouth. It will be a fairly accurate simulation, but it will not be real. If, however, you fully tune in to each of your senses as you eat, your experience will be slightly different from your mind's simulation. There will be errors in the simulation that will normally pass you by unnoticed. This means that the real treat, the one that you are eating in the present moment, will be far more wonderful because you are actually tasting it, rather than experiencing a simulation. All the interleaved nuances of flavours, aromas and textures will be experienced and savoured. They will be absolutely real, not an imitation. If, however, you do not pay attention, you simply will not notice the taste of your food – along with countless other things, such as the feel of the sun on your skin, the smell of freshly baked cakes, the smiles of loved ones, hugs and kisses, the laughter of children in the park ... The list is truly endless.

Thankfully, such losses are not inevitable because you can learn to pay attention in a very special way; a way that allows you to reconnect with the world around you. And when you do so, something astonishing happens. You begin to see the world in its true glory – full of magic, mystery and wonder. This is what this eight-week course offers; and it's so much more than the absence of anxiety, stress, depression and exhaustion. It offers you the opportunity to reclaim your life – to rediscover the simple, beautiful, *joy* of being alive.

A LIFE, RECONNECTED

The first step to regaining control over your life is learning to notice when your mind has begun to subvert itself and slip into unconsciousness. This is done by first training it to focus on one single thing at a time and then gradually learning how to move this 'spotlight of attention' around as you wish. You may not find it easy at first, but with gentle persistence, you can learn to see *where* the spotlight of attention is pointing, *when* it starts to wander away from your chosen focus, and then to bring it *back* to where you had intended it to be. And you do this by setting aside a few minutes each day with the sole aim of training the mind: seeing your attentional spotlight at work, and then bringing it back each time that it wanders away from your chosen focus.

To aid this process, it is helpful to have one place you can bring it back to, over and over again. You see, your mind is like a boat; it needs an anchor, so that it doesn't drift too far away from the shore with the ebb and flow of the tide. Meditation traditionally uses the breath as this anchor. For some meditators, the breath is sufficient, but for many (or when the mind is unusually scattered or busy) the breath may not be enough. People often need stronger and more noticeable sensations to focus on than those provided by the gentle to-ing and fro-ing of the breath. They need more options. This is especially true if you have breathing difficulties, or if distractions have become too intrusive.

If you have found the breath to be sufficient so far, don't worry – it will still be there for you later in the course. However, this week is dedicated to exploring alternative anchors (be they the feet, the hands or the feeling of contact with a seat or mat, or even an external one, such as sounds) to give you a taste of the different qualities that each one brings. If you have practised mindfulness in the past, particularly if you have read our previous book, *Mindfulness: Finding Peace in a Frantic World*, or taken a course based on it, some of the ideas will seem familiar. But there are many subtle but crucial differences, the primary one being that over the coming weeks, you will learn how to tune in to the vedana (or feeling tone) as you carry out the meditations. You will tune in to the different flavours of awareness as you carry out meditations that may seem familiar but are, none the less, different from those you have practised previously. These will deepen your experience and understanding. This is the kernel of what we want to share with you over the coming weeks: it has, for us, become a treasure trove of new insights from the most ancient of Eastern traditions, as well as modern psychology and neuroscience. They have transformed our understanding of meditation and we hope that they will do the same for you, too.

Can mindfulness do harm?

This is an important question. There is an old adage in psychology that a treatment with no side effects is inert. And indeed, between three and ten per cent of people undergoing any psychological treatment may find that they feel worse afterwards than they did before they started.[1] Active ingredients make a difference, and sometimes this won't be pleasant. Newspaper columnist Oliver Burkeman expressed it by saying that if you are using a hammer with enough strength to drive a nail into a wall, then if you hit your thumb, it will hurt.

In our experience, meditating can very occasionally make

people feel worse in two contexts. The first is when people find that a difficult or traumatic memory comes up during a meditation and it feels overwhelming. If this happens, it is important to acknowledge it, to open your eyes and reground yourself, and perhaps even pause the practice for a while. The second is when someone has got so much out of mindfulness practice that they start to practise too much, sometimes several hours a day and then find themselves crashing. The same advice applies: let it go for a while, seeking help from a meditation teacher if you need to.

Mindfulness can be seen as analogous to physical fitness training which can sometimes injure you – especially if you overdo it when your body is unused to it, but also even when you have taken every precaution or are very experienced. You do not then conclude, however, that physical fitness and exercise are bad for you – rather, that you simply need to pace yourself. The same is true for mindfulness meditation.

WHEN CHALLENGES ARISE

It can be especially painful when you have been practising meditation – and think you are getting to grips with your difficult emotions – to find yourself getting very sad, anxious or angry once again. For some, it can feel as if the meditation itself is making things seem more intense. Difficult moods, and the memories, daydreams, plans or worries that come with them, can assail the mind as if from nowhere. It can happen to anyone, but it is more likely to occur if you have suffered difficult and traumatic events in the past. Sometimes the feelings go as quickly as they arrive; other times they stick around, almost as if they have taken up residence in the mind and refuse to leave. Before you embark on Week One, therefore, it is important to know what you can do when such challenges arise, both in meditation and also in your daily life.

- Firstly, it's useful to remind yourself that we all differ in what we most need to cope with life, to live with ease, presence and kindness in the midst of our chaotic world. And each of us copes in different ways at different times in our lives. This book offers a range of ways to help you in these times and we hope you will experiment to see what is most helpful for you.
- Secondly, it's important to go at a pace that feels right for you. The practice of mindfulness involves becoming aware of the full range of your experiences. It undoubtedly opens your eyes to the beauties and pleasures of everyday life, many of which you may have forgotten, but it can also put you in close contact with some of your most difficult thoughts, feelings, emotions and impulses. Learning to respond wisely to these moments is central to all mindfulness courses. But what is often forgotten is that it takes time – a period of allowing that cannot be rushed through or ignored. Always try to remember, therefore, that it's perfectly fine to stop and start elements of the course as you choose. True healing, and learning, will often occur in the quiet moments between practices, so don't feel that these periods are wasted or that you are in some way 'giving up'. Learning to pause can be a valuable lesson in itself. Here are some specific things to look out for and ideas that you may find helpful.[2]

Sudden storms

Difficulties can arise at any moment of the day or night, not only while meditating, and can be overwhelming. When this happens, see if it's possible to be very gentle with yourself. Perhaps in that very moment, taking a few deeper breaths and allowing your attention to drop to the feet on each out-breath (see box, below[3]). As you do so, explore the sensations of contact between the feet and whatever is supporting them. This helps you to find 'solid ground' from which you are better able to make a choice about what to do next.

The Six-second Stress Reliever: Soles of the Feet Meditation[4]

- Stand with your feet shoulder-width apart and slowly and gently draw in a long, slow, breath.
- Breathe out slowly, naturally and, as you do so, drop your attention to the soles of the feet.
- Pay attention to all the different sensations as they rise and fall like waves on the sea. You might notice a feeling of pressure under the heels and the balls of the toes, maybe a generalised achiness or tingling all over your feet or, perhaps, patches of warmth, coldness or maybe a sense of moistness between the toes. You might not experience anything at all, so try not to pre-judge what you will find.

You can do this exercise over one breath (about six seconds) – but more will be better.

How can something so simple be so powerful?

When you switch attention away from your churning mind and towards the sensations in your body (such as your feet), you are not just changing *what* fills your mind, but the whole *mode* of mind: you are shifting from thinking mode to sensing mode (from Driven to Being mode). Driven mode is great at solving problems – let's not criticise it – but its main way of attempting to solve problems is to use its ability to do mental time travel: 'hurrying on to a receding future ... hankering after an imagined past' in the words of poet R. S. Thomas.[5] If you get stuck in a thinking loop, then more thinking won't stop it. It'll tend to bring up more bad memories and dangerous futures. This creates anxiety, stress and unhappiness and burns up energy. If instead, you switch away from the whole Driven mode, you also switch away from your troubles. Focusing on sensations does this because they occur only in the present moment.

Another way of entering the Being mode during difficult times is to pay attention to sensations in the body, by expanding the 'zoom lens' of your attention to your whole body, allowing the difficulty to be held in a larger space with the breath in the background. In such moments, try to remember that it's also perfectly fine to move your attention away from the body to things around you. You could intentionally look around and maybe name the objects that you see such as 'chair', 'rug' or 'picture', or you could focus on the sounds around you.

Difficulty when meditating

Sometimes upsets arise when you are meditating, especially when something troubling has recently happened to you or reminds you of past hurt. These troubles may seem to have been reactivated by the meditation itself, or perhaps it was different to the simple relaxation that you were seeking. At these times, it's good to remember that you have choices. There is no need to grit your teeth and continue meditating *through* extreme mental or physical discomfort. The aim of meditation is not to 'harden your heart', so that you disconnect and no longer feel fully alive or able to embrace life. Rather, you are training the mind to deal skilfully and tenderly with what troubles you. In these times, it's helpful to distinguish between your *willingness* and *capacity*.[6] So when a difficulty arises, you could try making a choice as to whether or not you are willing to stay a little longer to work with it. But even if you *are* willing, is this the kindest thing to do? Gently ask yourself: *Do I have the capacity, the energy, right now?* If you're too tired or upset, it's fine to leave the difficulty on one side for a while, until you feel more able to work with it. If you don't want to set it aside completely, try choosing *how close* you want to move towards it, perhaps staying just on the edges, or seeing it a little way off in the distance, or perhaps broadening your field of awareness to your whole body so it feels as though the difficulty is being held in a wider space. You could also try setting a time limit on how long you are willing to stay with it – say, five or ten breaths.

As you become more familiar with the meditations, and how to use the different anchors for your attention (the feet, contact with seat, hands or breath), try to understand that when difficulties arise, it is perfectly OK to leave your intended practice for a while and instead stay with your anchor. You can also do this if you lose your focus or drift away from it and need to re-gather your attention. You are also free to move between anchors or combine them. As you settle into focusing on your chosen anchor, try asking yourself: *Can I stay with these sensations even in the midst of this difficulty?* Be gentle with yourself. There is no rush. Do not try to be 'brave', to 'grin and bear the pain' or to push yourself too hard. Simply explore. As you do so, see if you are able to give the difficulty a sense of space. Try breathing with it; knowing that it's around but intentionally not rushing to engage with it. If you don't feel comfortable staying with your anchor, open your eyes and take in whatever is to be seen around you.

If things get too intense for you, then tune in to your body and ask, *How are my body and mind feeling right now, in this moment? What else is here? What's my best support right now?* And then, take a long, slow, deep breath in and out . . . and begin whatever you believe is the best way of supporting yourself, such as taking a break, opening your eyes or bringing your attention back to your anchor. And at any time, feeling free to revisit practices that are familiar from previous courses, and being prepared to move on when life seems to require a different approach.

Whatever happens during your practice, always try to remember that in the midst of difficulty it can feel as if you are truly alone; but you are not. Countless people have experienced the same difficulties as you and they will wish to help. If you find yourself struggling, gently pause for a while, then reach out to like-minded people either over the Internet or in real life. You may find the advice of an experienced meditation teacher to be helpful too. And remember that you can always reach out to a qualified medical or psychological treatment practitioner if your experiences become too difficult for you (see also Resources, page 258).

In this way, by exploring a range of options, you are finding new and flexible ways to respond wisely to the ups and downs of life. In being flexible, nothing of what you have learned from your past meditation practice is lost, but much is added that might benefit you and those around you.

For all these reasons and more, the first thing you will learn in this new programme is to steady and ground yourself. This will give you a 'place to stand', a vantage point from which you can explore the moment-by-moment unfolding of your experience.

Practices for Week One

- **Finding Your Ground Meditation** (page 67) to be done either for ten minutes twice a day (meditation 1.1) or twenty minutes once a day (meditation 1.2) . Once you are familiar with the instructions, use the minimal instructions (Mi) version (1.4) or the timing track with the sound of a bell every five minutes (1.5).

- **Finding Your Ground Meditation – thirty minutes.** On at least one day this week, meditate for thirty minutes using the 30-minute version (meditation 1.3) or the minimal instructions (Mi) version or the sound of bells (1.5).

- **Everyday Mindfulness Practice: Finding Your Ground When You First Wake Up** – each morning. See instructions in box on page 72. You can also use the audio guidance (1.6) for the first few days.

All meditations for this week can be found at littlebrown.co.uk/deeper-mindfulness/week-1

The meditations can also be found on the authors' website at franticworld.com/deeper-mindfulness

Finding Your Ground Meditation

Preparation

1. You can do this either lying down – on a mat or a rug – or sitting. If you're lying down, allow your legs to be uncrossed, with your feet falling away from each other, and your arms lying alongside and slightly away from your body. If you choose to sit, use a firm, straight-backed chair, or a cushion or meditation bench. If you're sitting on a chair, allow your feet to be flat on the floor with your legs uncrossed. See if it's possible for your hips to be a little higher than your knees by putting a cushion on the seat of the chair to lift your hips, so there's a sense of stability in the body as you sit.

2. Let the shoulders be relaxed and your facial expression soft. And whether you are sitting or lying, allow your eyes to close if that feels comfortable, or lower your gaze. If you prefer to have your eyes open, that's also fine – allow your gaze to settle softly on some object nearby.

Awareness of how things are, in body and mind

3. Take time to find a posture that best supports your intention to be really awake and present right now. And feel free to adjust your posture if you need to.

4. Spend some moments now becoming aware of the whole body, sitting or lying here, and aware of how things are for you right now: the weather pattern in your body

and mind: restless or calm? Awake or tired? Whatever's here. See if it's possible to allow things to be as they are.

The feet

5. When you're ready, gather your attention and move it to your feet, noticing any sensations there may be here when your attention arrives. Start with the sense of contact with the floor, your mat or the ground. What do you notice here? There may be tingling, vibration, a sense of pressure or of heat or coldness in the toes, in the soles and instep, in the heel.

6. When you're ready, expand the attention to take in the rest of the feet, too. As best you can, open to any and all sensations there may be right now, coming and going. Spend time noticing which are prominent and which are in the background; not looking for anything special to happen. If there are no sensations, simply register a blank.

7. And when the mind wanders, as it will do again and again, gently escort the attention back to the feet.

The contact with what's supporting you – the seat

8. At a certain point, deliberately let go of the feet and shift your attention to the sensations of contact with whatever you are sitting or lying on. If you are sitting, bring your attention to the contact with the seat … the sense of pressure, or tingling. Notice what's here right now. If you

are lying down, you may notice several points of contact: the lower legs, the buttocks and lower back, the shoulders and the head. Spend time paying attention to the different sensations of contact, bringing the attention back when it gets distracted, as it will from time to time.

The hands

9. Now let go of the sense of contact with seat or floor and come to focus on your hands. Perhaps notice sensations in fingers and thumbs, the palms of the hands, the backs of the hands and to the sense of contact between the hands and whatever is supporting them right now. Allow this sense of contact to be centre stage in awareness.

The breath

10. When you're ready, let go of the hands, and shift the attention to the sensations of the breath. Find one place where you notice the sensations as you breathe: this may be the tip of the nose or the nostrils or the back of the throat or the chest; or it may be the sensations created by the breath down in the lower abdomen, the area around the navel.

    Choose one place and rest your attention here. See what there is to be noticed, breath by breath. Notice the changing pattern of sensations with each breath – the rising of the in-breath, the falling away of the out-breath ... and the spaces in between. No need to control the breath in any way, allowing the breath to breathe itself. Gently bring the attention back when it gets distracted.

Choosing your anchor

11. And now, choose whether to stay with the breath or return your attention to the feet, the seat, the hands or, if you're lying down, the physical contact between the body and whatever is supporting you.

12. There's no right or wrong. Sense as clearly as you can what best helps your attention to focus right now, what helps you to ground yourself. And then, shift the attention to your chosen focus, and place your full attention here. Abiding here in this one place, open to any and all sensations in this place as best you can. Your place of grounding – of settling in; an anchorage for your attention.

13. From time to time, especially when your mind takes you away, again and again, to other things, remind yourself that this is not a mistake – this *is* the practice right now. For each time it goes away, and you notice it's gone, there's another chance to rediscover your anchor – whatever feels right to you: the feet, the seat, the hands, the breath; a chance to come back, coming home, finding your ground again and again.

Continue this practice by yourself for as long as you choose.

Ending

14. And as you come to the end, reminding yourself that, wherever you are throughout the day, and whatever you're doing, pleasant or unpleasant, it can make all the difference to become aware of the feet on the floor, the seat on the chair or of the sensations of hands or of the breath. Finding your ground in this way can give you a sense of space, choice and calm.

Tori found the idea of choosing her own anchor very useful. She'd tried meditating many times before and had always focused on the breath. When the teacher said there would be options – the feet, the contact with the seat or the hands – she thought that her feet would be best for her. But as the meditation unfolded, she found that focusing attention on her hands grounded her most of all. 'I found myself smiling,' she said. 'I realised that I'd been expecting one thing, but when I tried it, it turned out to be totally different to what I was expecting. It's only a small thing, but I guess I always have a pretty fixed idea about how things are going to be. That's not always correct.'

Tori's discovery might have been small, but it has an important message. As we saw in Chapter Two, the default option for the mind is to predict what is going to happen in the next moment on the basis of what has happened in the past. This works well in most instances, but, as she said, we wind up having fixed ideas about how things will turn out. So long as our experience does not differ too much from the prediction, there is little motivation to pay attention to the reality, so we don't bother.

Tori decided that she would take each meditation practice, day by day, as a new experiment, deliberately not pre-judging what she'd discover.

'As I was doing the meditations,' she said, 'I noticed how my anchor effortlessly changed from day to day. I don't think I'd have noticed that before. I found it a little strange. What was settling and grounding on one day wasn't the next. So I started to use a different anchor each day. Each one seemed "fresh" and gave me a stronger signal. At this early stage, I wanted things to be as simple and easy as can be, so a nice, clean, strong signal worked best for me.'

Dan found the same. 'I thought that my feet on the floor would be my preferred anchor. And I really appreciated the sensations of contact. But when my attention got to my hands, they felt alive, really tingling. There were so many sensations going on. One hand was being held lightly by the other, and the lightness of that touch was beautiful – as if my body was being kind to itself. I had never noticed that before. I felt a bit tearful, actually – such a surprise. The next day was different. My mind was all over the place. My feet and hands even seemed to be competing for which would become the anchor and I chose the feet – with the breath in the background. That really settled me.'

Everyday Mindfulness Practice: Finding Your Ground When You First Wake Up

Waking up from sleep can be a vulnerable moment for many people. There is a post-sleep torpor that can last a few seconds, or a few minutes, and because these sensations can imitate the feelings of sluggishness that come with being depressed, it can reactivate old and very unpleasant thoughts and emotions. Being aware that this is a vulnerable time can help you to see what is happening. If you need extra help, we have provided a short track (1.6) to use on two or three mornings this week. After this, see if you can continue by yourself for the rest of the week.

This practice invites you to bring your attention to how your body feels in the moments before you get out of bed. Notice any sensations, whatever they may be: feelings of heaviness, discomfort or fatigue; or lightness and energy. Notice how they change and flux in their own time. Pay attention to how you react to them: do you find yourself judging how you slept? Or wondering how the day will go? There is no need to get rid of thoughts or feelings. Simply notice them – and your reactions to them – tenderly and with compassion. Complete this short period of practice by bringing awareness to your breath, for a few mindful breaths.

What is surprising about Tori and Dan's experiences is that they are not from people who are new to mindfulness, but from those who have meditated for a long time. Devi had also been meditating on and off for ten years and found that for her, the breath seemed the most natural anchor. It was the most familiar and, in the beginning at least, helped to stabilise her wandering mind. But as the week progressed, and the meditation guidance became more familiar, she was able to notice sensations in her feet, seat and hands more easily. During the course of the week, her feet became a new and trusted ally in focusing the mind. 'I had always used the breath,' she said. 'So it was a lovely discovery.'

But Devi noticed something else, too: 'The feet, hands and the contact with what I was sitting on made it easier to remember to ground myself, and bring myself back when my mood or mind wobbled as I went through each day. I know that I'm vulnerable when I start to scroll mindlessly through social media. Or when I snap at my partner or at the children. Or when I keep putting things off. I can see how much damage I'm doing to myself and family through these old habits seizing control. It happens far more often than is healthy. It's like a tar-pit at the centre of my soul. Once in, I can't get out. Using the Finding Your Ground practice was good because it helped me bring myself back into my body. I've meditated for a long time, but this was different. It feels more forgiving ... like you can take it at your own pace. And using different anchors has been really helpful. Especially with my sense of disconnection ... which I now realise was because I was going round and round in my head, staying on the thinking highway. So this meditation gave me an "off ramp", so I could exit the thinking highway.'

Even at the end of the eight-week course, Finding Your Ground was a meditation that Dan returned to again and again: 'This ability to experiment with different anchor points really supported me. I was able to find a solid and stable presence within my body; a place where the mind didn't shout so loudly. These different parts of my body became quite familiar – like old friends – both on waking and also as I moved around during the day. Especially as I moved through my day. They allowed me to feel safe. So although I sometimes find that my mind still goes down the rabbit hole of brooding, I'm now much more likely to catch it when it does, and more able to coax it back out into the daylight afterwards.'

These benefits continued to accrue: 'In my daily practice, I now use the new anchors of feet, seat and hands. Especially the seat. It has helped me ground my practice in a very physical way and allowed me to settle more deeply on to my meditation bench and to check in with myself at various times during the day. This steadies and grounds me when things are getting too frantic.'

As you embark on the meditation practices for this week, see if you can remind yourself that the intention of the programme is not to get rid of all your thoughts or problems – or indeed, any of them. The Being mode of mind (see page 29) does not try to get rid of or 'solve' the feelings of being driven, exhausted and overwhelmed that may have brought you to this point. Instead, it cradles your racing mind and turbulent emotions in a warm, attentive presence. It's a form of awareness that clearly sees that many of our most distressing emotions are, in fact, the natural response of a mind trying its best to protect us in the only way it knows how. But these strategies often backfire. Mindfulness helps us to see this ever more clearly. It reveals how our minds become entangled and enmeshed; but, more importantly, it reveals what we can do about it. And often the best thing you can do is to do nothing at all; rather, just sit, surrounded by your own awareness, and let your mental tangles unfurl, all by themselves.

CHAPTER SIX

Week Two: Taking a Pause – Befriending and Gathering a Scattered Mind

The young couple were understandably excited. They'd just moved to a sturdy old farmhouse on the edge of Exmoor, overlooking the Doone Valley, out towards the Bristol Channel. It was to be their family home – but only after a lot of work. An awful lot of work.

Decorating was the easy part; the couple had a flair for design and many winter evenings to fill. Then, when spring arrived, it was time to plan their garden, a wilderness strewn with stones, weeds and thorn bushes. Once they'd decided where the flower beds and the vegetable patch would go, they set to work clearing and digging. All was going well – until they tried to move a big stone that was right in the middle of the space they'd planned for flowers. It was an enormous mass of solid slate. It would need both of them to shift it. They began digging around and underneath the rock, hoping to loosen it enough to roll it out of the way. But it was stuck fast, so they began using metal scaffold poles as levers. Still it wouldn't budge. They carried on scraping away, removing more and more earth, before realising that this stray stone was actually a rocky outcrop of the moor – the rock on which their house was built, and on which they were now standing.

'We need a road drill and an earthmover,' sighed one.

'Or we could make a rock garden with wildflowers,' said the other.

Trying to change ourselves 'for the better' can be like trying to dig up that stone. We assume that if we meditate long enough, or hard enough, then we will get rid of the parts of ourselves that we don't like. But what if the very things we want to change are not like a boulder that can be removed, but are, rather, akin to that rocky outcrop of mountain and moor? What if the 'flaws' we want to get rid of are, in fact, an inconvenient outcrop of a deeper and more fundamental aspect of our minds? An aspect that, underneath, is doing a lot of good work for us, trying its best to help us thrive in a seemingly chaotic world. Many of our self-styled 'flaws' can be like this. In one context they are the vital bedrock of our psyche, while in another they are seen as failings or even 'character defects'.

One 'failing' that can feel particularly irksome is a wandering mind; one that is prone to distraction and seemingly incapable of staying quiet during meditation. But such wandering isn't a flaw; it's a vital feature of the mind, and one that has been fine-tuned by nature to help us adapt and thrive in a constantly changing world. The mind's very distractibility ensures that we are also fast, creative and adaptable – qualities we all aspire to – helping us to walk a tightrope between chaos on one side and fossilisation on the other. And paradoxically, such distractibility arises out of the mind's ability to keep track of multiple simultaneous events while also consciously focusing on just the one. It does this by constructing multiple models of the world and refreshing them as new information arrives from the senses. The most dominant model then 'wins' and becomes our actual experience of the world. So even if you're focused on what's going on centre stage, a part of you is also aware of what's going on around the periphery. This means that the mind can be easily hijacked by things that appear on the edges of awareness – or by uncertainties that don't quite fit with its model of the world. We've mentioned some of these earlier, like a flickering TV screen in the corner of the eye or hearing your own name mentioned across a crowded room. When such unexpected things happen, attention shifts so that the mind can focus on the uncertainty to clarify it. We become distracted, in other words.

But distractions don't just crop up in the outside 'physical' world, but in our inner lives, too. This is because the same processes and algorithms are applied just as studiously to our internal data streams as they are to those from the outside world. And this process happens continuously, whether we are aware of it or not. Our minds are always active in the background, looking out for uncertainties and inconsistencies, areas of ambiguity and things that don't quite fit or make sense. Therefore, it spends much of its time mulling over the past, planning for the future and conjuring up multiple 'what-if' scenarios. The list is endless, rolling ceaselessly into the future.

By its very nature, much of this musing is vague and uncertain, and uncertainty is a magnet for awareness, especially if it involves intended actions that are yet to be completed.

Unfinished tasks, like unclosed files, are uncertain, so, just like a flickering TV screen, attention is drawn towards them. When this process of distracting works well, it becomes what we call 're-minding' – we are literally reminded of something. What's more, our attention *needs* to be capturable in this way because it reminds us of where we are in time and place – it helps us to organise our lives, keep track of our plans, appointments we've made, medicines we need to take and projects we need to complete. In an odd way, it's the distractions that help us keep track of our lives and of our sense of self. If you have a friend or family member with dementia, you will know how terrifying it can be when their mind stops giving them such timely reminders and they lose their sense of where they are in the world – and even of their own identity.

For the rest of us, though we may not like *where* the mind takes us when we get repeatedly distracted, we can still appreciate the underlying process, because it is doing important work, every moment of every day. Nevertheless, distractions can all too often become overwhelming in our hyper-connected fast-paced world. What worked well for our Stone Age ancestors, who lived in a far simpler world, has become a twenty-first-century curse. Which is why finding good anchors for attention is so important (and why we focused on it last week): it helps to strengthen the 'attentional muscles', so we can withstand the storms of anxiety, stress and despair that appear from time to time.

But what if there was a way of reducing the intensity of the storms themselves? With mindfulness, we can learn to do just this, by changing our relationship to the very stuff that threatens to overwhelm us. And building such a relationship is the theme of this week.

*

When you return to your chosen anchor in meditation, it is easy to believe that what took you away – whether it's planning for the future or remembering the past – is in some way the 'enemy' (like the stone in the garden from the beginning of this chapter) and that meditation is designed to help you 'get rid' of it. And if you can't get rid of it, well, then you have failed. This might trigger a sense of shame, too: as if you were a child just discovered doing something naughty or even downright wrong. For these reasons, we often hear people say: 'I can't meditate. I tried it once. I'm hopeless at it. My mind keeps wandering . . . I'm just no good at it.'

But what if mind-wandering was not the enemy of mindfulness but rather an ally? Imagine joining a gym and arriving on your first day to discover that it had no equipment. No exercise bikes, no cross-trainers, no weights or treadmills. Just an empty room. You would feel cheated – that you had wasted your money having signed up to the gym specifically because you needed those pieces of equipment. Even though you might not know how to use them all, or even understand their significance, you would still demand to know where all the fancy machines had gone.

Now imagine that your mind is like a mental gym. If you had a clear and empty mind, it would be like walking into that empty gym. There would be nothing to practise on. Thankfully, when you meditate, the gym equipment invariably comes to you. A thought, an image, a memory, a plan, a bunch of to-do lists, impulses to check or send messages, daydreams, broodings and worries . . . Mindfulness training is not a clever way of getting rid of these things. You actually *need* the mind's activity to carry out the practice. Learning the skill of paying attention, intentionally, moment by moment, without harsh self-criticism, needs something to practise on. And your mind, wandering off again and again, is just what you need. It's a bit like a puppy wandering off to bring you all sorts of objects from around the house that you had forgotten about. If this sounds like your mind, then you already have all that you need to begin your training. And you don't need to grit your teeth and attempt to stop the mind's activity. Far from it. As meditation teacher Helen Ma asks: what if you don't need to change things, but simply to 'switch on the light', so you can see the patterns of your mind more clearly?

Mindfulness, model-making and the default mode network

Since our first book was published in 2011, neuroscience has undergone a minor revolution, and with it, the understanding of how meditation achieves its remarkable effects.

Until relatively recently, it was believed that the brain and nervous systems merely reacted to stimuli, that the nerves did very little unless stimulated into action. Although scientists have had sophisticated scanners such as fMRI for several decades, this assumption of passivity – that the brain waits until it receives a stimulus – persisted. Why? It was because the main interest of these experiments was the processing that happens when a stimulus is given. Nobody thought to scan the brain when nothing was happening. You don't rent expensive scanner time, put people in them, then fold your arms and wait for the pictures to emerge. You have to get the volunteers to *do* something – a *task,* such as those involving memory or attention; and you also need to get them to do 'control tasks' to contrast the other ones with.

But after a while, researchers began noticing something

curious. Between tasks, when participants were resting, their brains were still active. They seemed to slip into a 'default mode'. This default mode is not like when you put your computer or TV into sleep mode, however. This mode is highly active. So even when you are resting, the brain is buzzing with wave after wave of activity. And it's become known as the default mode network.

This network continues working ceaselessly unless it is damped down by a task that demands more focused attention, at which point another network (the 'task' or 'executive' network) switches on. It had been the task network that most neuroscientists were interested in, until they started to see the significance of the default network. But it turns out that the brain is always working, just like the other major organs of the body, such as the heart, lungs and liver. As neuroscientist Lisa Feldman Barrett says in her book *How Emotions Are Made*, your brain's 86 billion neurons 'never lie dormant waiting for a jump-start'.[1]

What on earth is the default mode network *doing* with all this constant and unstinting activity? In short, Feldman Barrett says, it's making predictions. It's looking for patterns and completing them through simulation, using information from both the distant and the recent past to build mental models of the world, and to decide what action should be taken. Imagination, planning, mental inference, using memory of what has happened and what *might* have happened (known as counterfactuals) – all of this is being used to generate future plans and solve problems. And these models feed into the mind's overall global model – the model of reality that guides everything we think, feel, sense and do.

Researchers have found that when you are preoccupied by

brooding and worrying, the default mode network is highly active because brooding and worrying involve imagination. And when this happens, it's hard for the alternative task network to come online and to subsequently stay online. This is why last week you began exploring different anchors to help you find your ground – whether your feet, seat, hands or the breath. By doing this, you were giving yourself a *task* that gently inhibits the default mode network.

And it's why *this* week, you are ready to take another step: to build a different relationship with the activity of the default mode network. You'll do this inside the laboratory of your daily practice by taking a deliberate pause, seeing where the default mode has carried you off to and, then and there, bringing a new sense of appreciation, gratitude and even awe towards the mind.

To begin the process of changing your relationship to your wandering mind and its wild and uncertain storms, you will need to explore the very moment when you first realise that your mind has wandered away from your chosen anchor. This is done by consciously pausing for a few moments *right then and there*, so that you can see more clearly where your mind has gone. This will help you become more familiar with the activity of your mind, so that you begin to see its patterns, and the places it returns to, again and again. And if, in those few moments, you are also able to cultivate a sense of *gratitude* and *wonder* for your mind, and all that it does for you, you will begin the process of changing how you relate to yourself, so that you start replacing frustration with kindness. Such an approach does two things: it cultivates the mind because you are training yourself to step back and see its activity more clearly, and it cultivates the heart, so that you gradually learn to bring a sense of kindness towards the mind.

If you are an experienced meditator, taking such a deliberate pause may prove difficult because you may have become so adept at noticing when the mind has wandered away that you automatically bring it back to your intended focus. This can happen so fast, and so automatically, that it can be a difficult habit to break. This is especially true if you have spent years perfecting the skill of a speedy shift back to the breath. If you find this to be the case for you, then a deliberate pause may feel like a disruption to your practice, and you may even experience the unnerving tendency of being drawn back into your stream of thoughts. This may also trigger a worry that you will lose your basic meditation skills. But you should not be concerned. Those skills will still be there if you should need them in the future. In essence, this week's practices will help you explore new options, rather than close down old ones. You will learn to notice not only *when* the mind has been distracted but also *how* to use a pause to notice what your mind is doing; whether it is planning, daydreaming, remembering or worrying. And this, in turn, will help you cultivate a moment of gratitude for your mind.

Practices for Week Two

- **Taking a Pause Meditation** to be done for either twenty minutes (meditation 2.2) once a day or ten minutes (meditation 2.1) twice a day for five days. Once you're familiar with the instructions, please feel free to use the 'minimal instructions' (Mi) version (meditation 2.4), or simply use the one with only the sound of a bell at five, ten, fifteen, twenty, twenty-five and thirty minutes to help you choose the length of practice for the day.

- **Taking a Pause Meditation – thirty minutes** (meditation 2.3). On at least one day this week, sit for thirty minutes, using the most appropriate track.
- **Everyday Mindfulness Practice: Taking Pauses Through Your Day.** See instructions in box on page 99.

All meditations for this week can be found at littlebrown.co.uk/deeper-mindfulness/week-2

The meditations can also be found on the authors' website at franticworld.com/deeper-mindfulness

Taking a Pause Meditation

This is a meditation designed both to help you ground yourself in the present moment and to develop a different relationship to the mind when it wanders.

Preparation

1. You could do this meditation either lying down – on a mat or a rug – or sitting on a firm, straight-backed chair, or a cushion or meditation bench. Take time to find a posture that best supports your intention to be really awake and

present right now. Allow your eyes to close, if that feels comfortable, or lower your gaze.

Short body scan

2. When you're ready, gather your attention and, moving it to your feet, notice any sensations there may be here ... in the toes ... the soles and instep ... the heels ... and the top of the feet. Keeping the attention on the feet, notice any sensations, no matter how fleeting, as they appear. See how they come and go, changing moment by moment. Be curious, taking a friendly interest, whether the sensations are pleasant or unpleasant, remembering that there's no *right* way to feel.

3. Now, expand your attention slowly to take in the lower legs, the knees, then the thighs, until you are holding *both* legs in awareness. And now include the sense of contact of seat on chair, stool or cushion ... noticing whatever physical sensations there may be here.

4. Expand your attention again up the body to the pelvis and hips ... Then to the lower back and the lower abdomen and, moving up the body, to the chest in front right up to the collarbones, and up the back – right up to the shoulder blades, noticing all the physical sensations in the upper body.

5. When you're ready, expand your attention again – this time to include the left hand and arm ... then the right hand and arm ... then right across the shoulders ... the

neck ... and the face and head ... until you are holding the whole body in awareness.

6. See if it is possible to allow all the sensations in the body to be just as they are – letting go into this moment – fully present, here and now, with the body as it is.

Choosing an anchor

7. When you feel ready, focus your attention on one place in the body where you find it most easy to anchor your attention. This might be the sensations of the breath as it moves in and out of the body. Or, if you choose, you can focus on the contact of your feet on the floor, or your body on the chair or mat, or the contact of your hands with whatever is supporting them. Wherever you choose, simply sense what is here, moment by moment, as best you can.

Taking a pause: befriending and gathering the mind

8. Sooner or later, you'll probably find that the mind wanders away from your anchor to thinking, planning, remembering, daydreaming. When this happens, there is no need to criticise yourself; no need to 'rush back' to the breath. Instead, take a deliberate pause and see clearly where the mind has wandered to, perhaps saying inwardly, 'Here's thinking; this is what thinking is like' or, 'Here's worrying; this is what worrying is like', or, 'Here's planning; this is what planning is like.'[2]

9. See if it's possible to bring kindness to the mind, perhaps even marvelling at its ability to do its work; glimpsing a brief moment of gratitude for the mind doing the best it can.

10. Then gently escort your attention back slowly – taking your time to reground yourself before coming back to your intended focus, allowing sensations in the body to anchor you in the present moment.

11. Remind yourself that noticing that the mind has gone and bringing it back; this *is* the meditation – this *is* the practice right now – seeing the mind-wandering as an opportunity to cultivate patience and compassion as you bring the attention back, over and over again.

Ending

12. Remember that the body and breath are always available to you to help you take a pause … whatever's going on. They offer a place of stillness and peace in the midst of your day as it unfolds from moment to moment.

How did you find your session in the mind gym? Was it full of useful equipment that allowed you to explore your wandering mind in all its turbulent beauty? Or did you find the experience frustrating, leaving you with a lingering sense of despair? A vague feeling of unease, perhaps, because you didn't really manage to get started, let alone make progress? You'd begin, realise that your mind had wandered off, and then, even before you'd consciously paused to pay attention to your mind and body, your mind would leap off somewhere else? And so, time after time, your mind would wander off, before wandering off again and again.

This is normal. Your mind was simply behaving as minds are wont to do. It seems to have a mind of its own. Even so, you probably criticised yourself for your inability to cultivate a calm and clear mind. This criticism, too, is normal. It's your mind doing its best to spur you on to greater efforts.

Ella's experience surprised her. She said, 'My mind had wandered off, as it always does, and I began to criticise myself for it, as I always do, and then I just stopped. I managed to pause for just a moment rather than harshly yank my mind back to my anchor. And in that moment, just as my inner critic was about to leap into action, another little voice popped into my mind and quietly asked: "Has the judge in your head ever found you innocent?"'

'The answer was a resounding "No". *Not once*. My inner critic is always there in the background demanding perfection. Whatever I do, it's there, ready to bark criticism at me. Realising that it's always there, as a semi-independent "feature" of my mind, was a new and radical departure for me. What's interesting is that I've heard so many meditation teachers say you shouldn't be judgmental when you come back from mind-wandering. But it never really sank in. I would always drift back into judging. It's my default. This meditation gave me actual practice at doing the opposite of judging. Not only the pause, and being grateful, but slowing down the journey back.

'Following a struggle early on in the week, I decided to do the minimal instructions practice and bypass my feet and legs (I get pain in my legs a lot). This turned out to be one of the more

peaceful sittings of the week. I found that after the brief instructions, I could quite easily move back to focusing on the breath.
In the past, I found long silences rather daunting, so this in itself
was a bit of a breakthrough for me. Doing it this way also helped
me to appreciate the guidance about not rushing back when you
realise that your mind has wandered. I'm normally so full of
recriminations, so that little pause was enough to remind me to
be compassionate and forgiving of myself. Those few moments of
silence and forgiveness were enough for my mind to truly relax,
so that I could then gently coax it back to focusing on my breath.'

What's going on here? When you begin to treat your mind
with appreciation rather than forcing it to behave a certain
way, it starts to settle down of its own accord. The pause and
the gratitude change the mind's perspective. You find yourself
being less judgmental and this frees up more space in the mind
because you are not trying to get busy solving the 'problem' of
a wandering mind. Your mind isn't getting into needless battles
with itself. This is a real advantage when you want your mind
to be clear and focused (see below and box, page 94).

The practice of pausing and sensing – how does it help?

Laboratory tests show that those who practise mindfulness are
better at focusing and sustaining their attention and are less
distractable.[3] Meditation training enhances the brain rhythms
that play a critical role in filtering and optimising the flow of
sensory information.[4] Bringing these skills into your everyday
life can be transformative, especially if you suffer from stress,

depression and exhaustion. This is because it helps depressed people overcome the attention and memory problems that accompany depression.[5] In particular, sufferers often have difficulties with filtering out distracting stimuli,[6] in disengaging from distractions[7] and in learning how to discriminate between genuinely important and pressing matters and irrelevant and less pressing ones (that is between the 'signal' and 'noise').[8] Mindfulness teaches new skills to help deal with these issues.

There is a part of the brain called the anterior cingulate cortex (ACC) that is responsible for monitoring tasks and keeping things on track. The ACC has links both to the parts of the brain concerned with emotion (the limbic system) and to those involved with the 'cognitive control' of tasks (the prefrontal cortex). A study asked experienced meditators to practise focused-attention meditation inside a brain scanner. Participants pushed a button whenever they noticed their minds had wandered. The study found that the moment they became aware of mind-wandering corresponded to increased activity in the ACC.[9]

As the mind starts to wander during meditation, the ACC plays an important role in detecting that it is not where you had intended it to be and then feeds this information back to executive-control networks so that attention can be refocused. Studies have shown improvements in ACC functioning after people learn to meditate.[10] The better functioning of the ACC means that you are able to see your mind-wandering earlier and to make a smooth adjustment without having to be harsh towards yourself and be self-critical.

Mindfulness practice helps you to focus on one thing at a

time, and to deal more skilfully with your mind when it does get distracted. Mind-wandering is the 'gym equipment' that gives you lots of chances to learn how to relate to your mind with kindness and gratitude rather than self-criticism (which just creates more distraction).

But this is all too often easier said than done, as Ana found out: 'I found marvelling at my own mind very difficult. I was taught in meditation classes that when the mind wanders, "Yeah OK, that's what minds do, so gently but *firmly* bring it back to the breath." But with these meditations we were being asked to go further; to pause, to marvel and then to return. I found this so difficult. When I began to pay more attention to the actual meditation instructions, I realised that I had been bringing in ideas from my previous meditative practices and not following the spirit of these new ones. So I gently dropped these old ideas from my mind. I also realised that I had been misinterpreting the word "firmly" (which didn't even feature in this meditation). I'd been thinking of it in terms of "tough" or "harshly" – kind of like a too-strong bear hug. I then realised that "firmly" could also be like a warm, loving and protective embrace – a kind of firm but gentle strength. Once I realised this, I was able to drop the idea of "firmly" from my mind and instead bring a more loving, caring and compassionate attitude towards it. My concerns simply fell away after that.'

Occasionally, in the midst of a meditation that appears to be going 'well', an unpleasant memory or feeling might crop up. It's almost like a switch has been tripped in the mind, or like a nerve or muscle has been unexpectedly snagged, sending a sharp pain through the mind or body. This happened to Jess when an unpleasant memory appeared during the practice, something that she felt guilty about.

'How could I bring a sense of appreciation or wonder to my mind when it was bringing up this horrible memory?' she asked.

Something similar happened to Sim during Week Two. It was triggered not when he was meditating but when he caught a glimpse of himself in a shop window as he walked through town. 'I thought to myself, *You look ridiculous; trying to look cool and you're not. You know that, so why do you try so hard?* This brought back a lot of feelings from my teenage years. From when other kids would tease me. When I feel like this, it's just impossible to be grateful to my mind. It just makes me feel a little broken and useless inside.'

In scenarios similar to those experienced by Jess and Sim, your mind – even though it's shouting harshly at you – still thinks it's helping you. You can probably think of occasions when shouting at someone might be understandable, such as a child about to step into a busy road. Perhaps you have had the experience of being shouted at in such situations, or have suffered the anger of a parent, teacher or peers over the longer term? From such experiences, or an instinctive fear of failure, you might end up with the ingrained habit of harsh self-criticism that takes the form of shouting inwardly at yourself. In most circumstances, such shouting backfires miserably. It stops you from acting effectively by narrowing your attention, dampening your creativity and generally making you feel worthless for no benefit whatsoever. Yet many of us still persist with such tactics, just like Jess and Sim.

On these occasions, it might be a little unrealistic to try and bring a sense of wonder and gratitude to your mind. Instead, see if it is possible to bring in a little kindness, turning with compassion towards the imagined urgency that it is creating. It might help to say inwardly: 'It's OK not to like this. No action needed right now.' We'll come back to this approach in more detail in Weeks Four and Five.

Can mindfulness enhance intelligence?

The Graduate Record Examination (GRE) is a standardised test often required for admission to graduate programmes in the USA. Psychologists Michael Mrazek, Jonathan Schooler and colleagues[11] studied the effects of a daily mindfulness practice on performance on GRE verbal-reasoning tests after two weeks of practice in class, forty-five minutes a day, four times each week. Each mindfulness class included a ten- to twenty-minute practice of focused attention, with instructions to allow the mind to rest naturally rather than trying to suppress thoughts. Students also practised for ten minutes a day outside class.

They also compared the GRE scores for these students against those of others who were randomly assigned to spend the same amount of time each day learning about nutrition, rather than meditating, and logging their food intake at home during the week. All students in the study also completed a psychological test assessing their working memory, including a measure of how much their mind wandered (that is, thoughts that were not related to the task in hand).

The results showed that those who had practised mindfulness had higher scores on the GRE (equivalent to a 16 per cent increase in score) compared to those allocated to the nutrition group. Importantly, the researchers found that the higher scores were due to the students in the mindfulness group experiencing less mind-wandering after they had practised the meditation (especially those whose minds were prone to distraction before they learned to meditate). The marked effect on performance was due to being able to move around things they had found difficult, rather than brood about them. This released the students' mental capacity to focus on later test items without distraction. Mindfulness may not make you more intelligent, but it allows the intelligence you already have to shine through.

There is a deeper aspect to all this, too. When Jess and Sim looked a little more closely at what was happening in their minds, they noticed that there were two sides to it: there was the unpleasant memory that appeared in the mind as if from nowhere – the initial distraction; and there was the reaction to those memories. 'When I first became aware of the storm in my mind, I took a closer look at it,' said Jess. 'And I remembered what my meditation teacher had told me. She said that I had no control over what appeared in my mind, but I did have control over what happened next. I could then see my reaction to that initial memory much more clearly. I realised that I could use such moments to learn to respond rather than react. So that's what I did. As soon as my inner critic fired up and began attacking me for the idea of even *trying* to bring appreciation and wonder into my mind, I consciously took a deep breath and relaxed into the criticism. I quietly said to myself, "Thank you for trying to protect me." I realised that my inner critic had been reminded of painful past events and was trying to spur my mind into action – to raise its shields and ready its defences. All for me. Which was quite kind of it, I began to think. So once I acknowledged this – acknowledged the distraction, and that I had been successfully reminded of my painful past – the inner critic had done its job, so then it fell silent. Absolutely silent. It was weirdly effective. I was then able to bring in a little compassion, not only for myself, but also for my inner critic. After that, each time my inner critic went on the rampage, I gently acknowledged its concerns and contin- ued with my meditation. What was more transformative for me, though, was bringing this attitude to my daily life. Each time the critic appeared, I simply acknowledged the distraction, its concerns, and it fell silent. So instead of my days being consumed by battles with myself and those around me, I began to live a slightly more harmonious life. Oh, sure, there were still battles, but they were less frequent, far less vicious and certainly shorter.'

Another approach was taken by Mira: 'I used to chair lots of committees. In many of these meetings there was often somebody who was angry or critical about everything. They'd interrupt all the time, so that it was impossible for the commit- tee to focus on its task. They tended to dominate the meeting to such a degree that people would be afraid of them. I often found myself hoping that they wouldn't turn up to the meetings. It wasn't very pleasant at all. After a while, I learned to just say, "Thank you very much, now would anyone else like to speak?" From time to time, they would start up again and I would just say, "Thank you, we've heard what you have to say. Is there anyone else?" In this way, everything settled down. I learned that in the end, most committee members like and respect fairness – the sense that everyone should be heard – even the difficult ones.

And often when the person with the loud voice stopped speaking, a quieter person would speak up and help to move things forwards in a way that helped the meeting. So now when I find the "committee in my head" being distracted and dominated by the inner critic, I say gently but firmly, "Thank you, I've heard your opinion, now is there anyone else who'd like to speak?" It's amazing how often this takes the wind out of its sails, and a quieter, kinder voice can be heard.'

Spacious
by Kaveri Patel

Dear you,
you who always have
so many things to do
so many places to be
your mind spinning like
fan blades at high speed
each moment always a blur
because you're never still

I know you're tired
I also know it's not your fault
The constant brain-buzz is like
a swarm of bees threatening
to sting if you close your eyes

You've forgotten something again
You need to prepare for that or else
You should have done that differently

What if you closed your eyes?
Would the world fall
apart without you?

Or would your mind
become the open sky
flock of thoughts
flying across the sunrise
as you just watched and smiled

Ana liked this poem. It reminded her of herself and gave her hope for the future. She had struggled through Week One and did the same through the first half of Week Two. Until, finally, something changed:

'I thought to myself, I've struggled and bulldozed my way through these meditations and tried to make them work. But I didn't get what I was looking for. I was just as grumpy and stressed as ever. Then I realised that I hadn't really engaged with the spirit of the practices. I had been following the instructions to the letter but not actually engaging with their inner values. So I thought to myself, It's worth the experiment. I will try pausing, then marvelling and regrounding myself for the rest of this week. I will engage with the spirit of these ideas.

'From previous experience, I know that extending generosity, compassion and kindness towards myself has been life changing during the few times I've managed to do it. But I have some really horrible memories, so the challenge for me was extending that same kindness to these. It was hard, but gradually, something did seem to change. Knowing that I could take a break at any time really helped me with this. What allowed me to take a different perspective on it all was realising that my mind may have been bringing up those memories for a reason but that didn't mean that I then had to build on them and make the situation worse. I didn't have to let them take over my life and define me as a person. Yes, those horrible things had happened – they were a part of my history – but they were only one small part of me, not the whole of me.

'There was a moment towards the end of Week Two when I felt a deep bliss which gave me a calmness that I haven't felt for a long time. I felt really "present", to a degree that I haven't felt before. It was quite amazing; I felt the benefits of the practice and resolved to continue to let go of all my self-judgments about being a bad person – well, as best as I could, anyway. I have to say that later in the week, I noticed self-judgments settling in again, and then some disappointment about not being able to maintain the earlier sense of relaxation. Thoughts about "how much better I should be by now". Then I caught myself and realised that I was getting drawn into the vortex and managed to climb out much quicker than I used to.'

Everyday Mindfulness Practice: Taking Pauses Through Your Day

This week, see if you can take pauses throughout the day to tune in to the sense of the world around you. Focusing on a different 'sense door' each day (taste, sight, touch, smell and hearing), spending a few moments registering sensations and whether they are pleasant, unpleasant or somewhere in between. It may help to keep the sensations of breathing or your feet on the ground in the 'background' of awareness as you do so.

- Day 1: Taste What's the feeling tone of the first sip of your first drink of the day? Or the taste of your breakfast or midday meal – the first mouthful, perhaps? And what about the other mouthfuls?
- Day 2: Sight Noticing what your eyes take in around you as you move or sit. Taking a pause to notice whether it is pleasant, unpleasant or more neutral.

Then on the next days, too, taking pauses as you go about your daily life to focus on each sense, noticing what you are 'taking in' in that very moment; and, before the moment fades, seeing if you can notice whether it is pleasant or not:

- Day 3: Touch
- Day 4: Smell
- Day 5: Hearing

Feel free to record your experiences on paper in your journal or diary when you get the chance to do so.

COMING TO YOUR SENSES EVERY DAY

How did you find the practice of re-engaging with your senses? Was it difficult? Eye-opening? Invigorating? Or a mixture of all three? Noah found that some senses were more difficult to engage with than others. Sight and hearing were easier for him: 'They always feel "right here",' he said. 'But I had to deliberately focus on *taste*. It felt like there was more of a distance between me and it. This meant that tasting even the most familiar of things took me to places I don't naturally go. Deliberately tasting my coffee, for example. Then I noticed something else that was really quite profound. When I noticed one thing – really noticed it – everything else became more vivid as well, not just the sense I had been focusing on. This came home to me on the third or fourth day, when I was walking through some woodland and decided to focus on my sense of hearing. I heard the wind rustling through the leaves, the songs of numerous little birds and the creaking of the trees. Then I noticed the smell of the woodland. I could smell dozens of different aromas – the earth, the "resinous" smell of pine needles, even the moistness of the air. So what I'd thought of as one smell was actually far more complex, with countless different layers to it. I wasn't just engaging with my sense of hearing but also with all my other senses. I suddenly felt connected to the woodland – almost becoming a part of it – because *all* my senses were reaching out to connect with the world around me. I don't think I've experienced anything like that before – at least not since I was a child, when everything seemed new and magical.'

Noah's experience is important because it highlights the mental blocks that can prevent a sense from having its full impact. Remember Chapter Two, where we revealed that the brain *predicts* what you'll sense? Intentionally switching your attention back to your senses places the predictive mind on the back burner, while simultaneously bringing you back into the present moment *as it is*. Once you pay full attention to a single sense, the predicting mind temporarily recedes into the background, allowing you to automatically reconnect with your other senses as well.

This was Ana's experience: 'By allowing myself to be aware of what's going on – of what I am seeing, hearing and smelling – I also felt more connected to everything else, too. So I've begun experiencing a lot more of my life just by connecting with the tiny things, just by focusing on them. This week, I saved the life of a bee that had become trapped in the corner of a room. Normally, I wouldn't even have noticed it, but I was focusing on my hearing at the same time, so I heard its frantic buzzing. It's amazing what you normally miss.'

And Jess: 'Last Sunday we went for a long walk. My partner isn't quite as fit as he used to be and struggled a bit. I usually get quite annoyed at having to wait or slow down. Then I feel guilty about getting cross. This time I stopped "waiting" and thought, *Here's a good chance to do the everyday mindfulness and simply take in the sights and sounds.* The more I did this, the more I actually appreciated where I was. I was amazed at my surroundings, and then something else, too – the sense of just observing my surroundings brought a stillness to me. It was quite profound. I now see what people mean when they say that mindfulness is not about searching for big transformations or some kind of enlightenment. It's in the subtleties. And the coming together of these small realisations – well, they build on one another, until you reach a point of calm awareness.'

As in so many other areas of mindfulness, you can be aware of a concept but still not manage to find the motivation or time to put it into practice. This usually happens because the mind has seemingly more pressing matters to deal with. And to be fair, that is its job. The predictive mind always has a long list of projects to work through, so if you finish one, that's just the cue to start the next.

Focusing directly on your sensations gives you a break from this litany of 'things I must do'. This simple step not only results in greater sensory pleasure, but also rekindles feelings of curiosity, wonder and awe. And, often as not, when your Driven mode has calmed down a little, you also find that you have more time and energy to make intentional choices about what you would truly like and need to do next.

As you carry out these practices, you may notice that some things are pleasant on one occasion and unpleasant on another. For example, going for a hike can be wonderful but, ultimately, tiring. Going to a concert or a club is a sensory feast – for a while. So much happens from moment to moment that it's easy to see how pleasant and unpleasant sense experiences can become mixed up and change from moment to moment. This is the kernel of this practice. It progressively teaches you that such 'micro-moments' unfold as they will, each one triggering feeling tones of pleasant, unpleasant and neutral. In one moment, you might notice something pleasant and then a different 'sense door' opens up and this may feel unpleasant. You might enjoy the flavour of your favourite drink while simultaneously feeling a ripple of unpleasantness if it is too hot or too cold, too sweet or not sweet enough, or perhaps too strong tasting or weak and insipid. Often, you will not notice such nuances because your reactions are automatic. You can too easily be buffeted about by the constantly changing feeling tones without fully realising it. Nevertheless, what you like or dislike has profound effects on you, whether you see, hear, taste, smell or touch them. By becoming aware of them, and the effects they have on you, you can learn to consciously respond rather than react.

Or, as Ana said: 'I became so much more aware of beauty. The world is full of beauty if you take the time to notice. I began to notice the stars in the evening, seeing and hearing birds in the garden and even the dew drops on the washing line. They were especially exciting because I became aware of them in such familiar spaces as my garden. It's a little city garden that I'm now totally in awe of.'

CHAPTER SEVEN

Week Three: Rediscovering the Feel of Things

Gwyneth is ninety years old and enjoys keeping apace with tech. She was sitting in her favourite armchair by the window with an intense look on her face as she squinted at her iPad.

Then the iPad emitted a series of loud clicks.

'Aargh – not again!'

Gwyneth loves that her iPad takes photos but grumbles that it's often 'too clever', taking a long sequence of photographs in the space of a second. Such 'photo bursts' happen whenever she holds one of its buttons for a moment too long. She often does this by accident, only later realising that she has captured fifteen near-identical pictures of her chair, her lap, the tip of her nose or the wall across from where she is sitting. Before she can even begin to think about stopping it, these photos are uploaded to her media library and the device forms a new 'memory' for her, all put together with a soundtrack from one of her playlists. And occasionally, a little dialogue box will pop up and ask, 'Is this you?'

Our mental models of the world are a bit like this. But there is one critical difference: although the first image in a mental photo burst might be based on solid data from the 'real' physical world, subsequent ones are *internally* generated, based on matching up that first image with sequences of similar ones from your own past. As the mental photo burst unfolds, the images *may* be updated by comparing the internal pictures with the actual data arriving from your senses – but they may not be. If the actual data from your senses isn't strong or precise enough to contradict the photo burst, then your conscious experience will arise solely from your internally generated pictures, not from what you are perceiving. It's almost as if two parallel information streams are flowing through the brain: one contains raw data coming in from the senses; the other, a virtual video stream. This virtual stream, a rapid sequence of mental models, is constructed from predictions of what is likely to happen from one moment to the next, based upon what's happened in the past. If this seems difficult and complicated, well, it is. Astonishingly so. But it is still easier than the brain relying on completely new data. Processing new data takes more effort than relying on old data.

The effects of this can be seen in daily life. If you are walking down a street, the chances are you will not feel your actual feet on the ground. Instead, your experiences will be running off a virtual mental loop created from your predictions of what it normally feels like to walk. And usually, you will be none the wiser. In fact, you will only become aware of this virtual world should you make a mistake, such as when you step off a pavement and stumble, and then discover that what you thought was the edge of the kerb was, in fact, a white line. Your brain took in the information (the white line), the photo burst predicted that it was a kerb, and then you stumbled over nothing. We have all experienced this countless times but think of the implications: if it had been a real kerb, rather than a white line, the experience of stepping down would have come from your predictive model rather than from your actual sensations. But you stumbled instead, which forced you to reconnect with the real physical world, if only for a few seconds, before your mind began to seamlessly construct an updated model. That little mistake was a moment of reconnection with the world; perhaps one of only a handful that day.

The brain can only work this way, relying on virtual models, because our world is almost always predictable. The brain has only to sum up the probabilities from the past, generate a photo burst from the initial data, and occasionally check in with the data stream, correcting where necessary. Such mental models feel true and familiar because they are constructed from your own past. They are personal, intimate, which makes them feel overwhelmingly compelling. Despite this, with a little effort, it *is* possible to draw aside the veil and observe the actual world as it unfurls 'frame by frame'.

Remember in Chapter Three we learned of Eadweard Muybridge's work and how he managed to prove that galloping horses really do lift all four hooves off the ground as they run (see page 30)? This was only possible because he managed to take a series of pictures that captured the actual data – the feet of the galloping horse, frame by frame. He slowed everything down to stillness, to reveal the underlying patterns of movement. Well, this week you will learn to look at your own experiences in a similar way. The following practices will progressively reveal the very first moment that something arises in your experience, showing, frame by frame, how the reactivity pulse in the mind then creates its virtual world based on the feeling tone. They will demonstrate how your inner world is built upon moments that feel either pleasant, unpleasant or neutral. Moments that you do not control but which, none the less, sculpt each moment of your whole life and your approach to the world. Moments that lead to future moments. It is *these* subsequent moments that can be guided and, ultimately, changed. For this to happen, you will need to go 'upstream' to register what happens in the first moment that a thought, feeling or sensation arises. You will explore what it is like to notice your experience frame by frame. You will learn to see the first inkling of a feeling. Not a feeling in the sense of a 'fully grown' emotion, such as sadness or excitement, worry or relaxation, but a simpler sense of the 'pleasantness' or 'unpleasantness' of a moment. This simple sense *is* the feeling tone, the vedana, of a moment. To get a first taste of this, try the exercise below.

The feel of things

Look at the boxes overleaf. As you look at each one in turn, see if you can register how it *feels* to you; pleasant, unpleasant or neutral. There's no right or wrong answer, no need to think too hard. Your first reaction is fine.

A greasy frying pan

A smiling baby   The smell of drains

Sunshine on the beach

The smell of toast   The rustle of leaves

A spilled rubbish bag

A messy room   Freshly baked bread

What did you notice? Most people say that even *imagining* freshly baked bread feels pleasant. They instinctively know that they like it. They don't have to think about it for a long time. Conversely, most people have little trouble saying that they don't like the smell of drains. Once again, it's an immediate reaction. Of course, people differ in what they find pleasant or unpleasant, and in how *strong* the pleasant or unpleasant tone of a thing is, but it can still be detected.

We don't need to know exactly *how* we know the feeling tone, or how powerful it is, we just get an immediate sense or 'read-out' of whether something is pleasant, unpleasant or neutral. We get a 'felt sense' of it.

Such experiences are not static. The same experience can be pleasant on one occasion and unpleasant on another. For example, the rustle of leaves may be pleasant when walking through the woods on a sunny autumnal day. The very same rustling sound may be unpleasant if you think there's an intruder in your garden. Such differences can be significant and show the importance of not assuming in advance what you are about to discover. It is also important to realise that it is not possible to change the actual *feel* of your feeling tones as they arise. You cannot train yourself to register an *unpleasant* feeling as *pleasant*. They just *are*. But you can learn to change what happens next. You can learn to stop your feeling tones from triggering cascades of negative thoughts, feelings, emotions and even physical sensations. For if you learn to be *aware* of these feeling tones, you can then come to see more clearly the effects they have in the moments that follow; and it is these subsequent moments that you can respond to differently. You can learn to stop the feeling tones from triggering the instinctive, habitual reactions that mar so much of life. For it is your subsequent reactions – the reactivity pulses – that really do the damage. As you will recall from Chapter One, it works like this:

Things that feel *pleasant* tend to lead, in the very next moment, to an entirely natural wish for them to remain and to be a little fearful that they will fade away. Such feelings can trigger a sense of longing, of wistfulness, and a subtle sense of insecurity. These can lead to the first stirrings of anxiety and stress, and to feelings of emptiness and isolation. It's then entirely natural to want to cling even more tightly to the embers of your initial happiness and to crave the return of pleasant feelings.

Conversely, things that feel *un*pleasant tend to produce a sense of 'aversion', a desire to push them away, to run and to hide and to resist the feelings. This creates tension and stress, anxiety and fear, unhappiness and exhaustion. It may also trigger feelings of injustice, so that you start to feel like you're being picked on and bullied by life.

Events that feel neither pleasant nor unpleasant tend to be followed by the mind 'tuning out'; feelings of boredom, nihilism and even disconnection may then appear. This can trigger a search for more stimulation. Something, anything, that can deflect the feelings of pointlessness. So even neutral feeling tones can tip you into a downward emotional spiral.

Feeling tones occur continuously, rising and falling like waves on the sea, so in practice, one is quickly superseded by another and then another in a seemingly endless cycle of little highs, lows and nothingness. This ensures that the mind is inherently self-correcting while also being nimble and creative. But just occasionally, things can start to go wrong. Over the coming weeks, we'll learn a little more about the ways that this can happen, but more importantly, you will learn how to correct the balance so that you can once again begin to live a happier, more contented and peaceful life. The first step along this road is learning to observe your feeling tones as they arise, frame by frame.

Practices for Week Three

- **Feeling-tone Meditation** – to be carried out for ten minutes twice per day (meditation 3.1) or for twenty minutes once a day (meditation 3.2). On at least one day this week, you should meditate for thirty minutes (meditation 3.3). Once you're familiar with the instructions, it will be worth using either the minimal instructions (Mi) version of the meditation (3.4) or simply practising for your chosen period of time using the sound of bells track. You might also keep notes in your diary (or journal) of any discoveries, delights or difficulties that you found with the meditations. In total, these Feeling-tone Meditations should be practised on at least six days out of the next seven.

- **Everyday Mindfulness Practice: An End-of-day Reflection on Feeling Tone.** At the end of each day, set aside a little time to allow the day's events to appear in your mind and notice the feeling tone of each one. See the box on page 120 and/or you can use audio meditation 3.5 for the first few days to get you started.

All meditations for this week can be found at littlebrown.co.uk/deeper-mindfulness/week-3

The meditations can also be found on the authors' website at franticworld.com/deeper-mindfulness

In the following Feeling-tone meditation, you will be first invited to 'ground' yourself in your breath and body and then to move your attention from sensations on the surface of your body, then to sensations inside the body, then to sounds and then to any thoughts or emotions that arise in the mind. The aim is to note the feeling tone of whatever appears. So if you are thinking about an upcoming holiday, or you hear a bird singing, you might register *pleasant*. Or if a noisy truck passes outside, or you feel a pain in your back, you may register the feeling tone as *unpleasant*. There is no need to think too hard, or even to know *how* you know it. The idea is to just register the sense of it: pleasant, unpleasant or neutral. On occasion, you may find that there is no feeling tone at all: this is fine – there's no need to sense something every time. If something happens, a sound or a thought, and you don't quite know if it is – or was – pleasant or unpleasant, there is no need to think too hard about it or to worry. There will be another one along in a moment. When you do register a feeling tone, it is not necessary to only use the words 'pleasant', 'unpleasant' or 'neutral'. Instead, you can use your own words to describe the feel of things, such as 'bitter-sweet', 'liked or 'disliked'.[2] Try out different words to describe your feeling tones and see what feels right for you. Alternatively, you could imagine a dial with a pointer that moves to the left or to the right, or perhaps a coloured dial with red to one side, signalling unpleasant, and green to the other, signalling pleasant. Registering feeling tones can be done in many different ways. Just as some people are 'visual' people in the way that they primarily relate to the world, and others are 'tactile', we all have slightly different ways of registering feeling tones. You could perhaps use the first day's practice to see which one works for you. Nevertheless, for the purposes of this book we will stick to pleasant, unpleasant and neutral.

Feeling-tone Meditation

Preparation

1. Settle in to sit, on a chair or a stool or a cushion. Allow the shoulders to be dropped and the head balanced, so that your posture embodies a sense of being present, awake for each moment. Then choose an anchor as in Weeks One and Two – the breath, feet, contact with seat or hands.

2. When you feel ready, deliberately expand the focus of your awareness to the whole body.

Feeling tone of body sensations and of sounds[3]

3. As you sit here, bring your awareness to whatever sensations in your body are most distinct at any moment, seeing if it's possible to register if they are pleasant, unpleasant or somewhere in between. For many sensations, the feeling tone may be quite subtle, so don't worry if you aren't sure; simply let go and wait for another sensation to arrive.

4. When you feel ready, expand the attention to sounds as best you can, registering the tonality of the sound – pleasant, unpleasant or neither? There's no need to think too hard about this; simply register what the body and mind already feels when a sound is received.

Feeling tone of distractions

5. At a certain point, when you feel ready, let sounds fade into the background and return attention to your anchor.

6. Whenever you find that the mind has become distracted, as soon as you notice this, see if it's possible to also notice the feeling tone of the distraction (just as you did with body sensations and sounds). It may be from something happening outside, or from inside your body or from your mind (a memory, or plan, or daydream, or worry) … whatever it is, when you become aware of it, take a moment to get a sense of whether it's pleasant, unpleasant or neutral.

7. And then, when you have registered the feeling tone, bring the attention back to the body. Come back and anchor yourself once again in this moment. And when the next distraction arises, once again register *its* feeling tone, before coming back to your anchor. Remember not to try too hard – if something is hard to register, let it go, and wait for something else to arise.

8. And sit in silence as you continue to do this practice on your own, checking in from time to time to see where your mind is, and noting the pleasantness or unpleasantness of wherever it had gone.

9. And remember that if anything seems overwhelming at any time, you can always let go of registering tonality and bring the focus of your attention back to your chosen anchor.

Ending

10. For the last few moments of the sitting, come back to focus on your chosen anchor, back to the simplicity of sensations, arising and dissolving from moment to moment.

Drew struggled through the first few days of Week Three. He found it difficult to avoid judging his feeling tones, even though his meditation teacher had spent a lot of time meticulously explaining how to register them, rather than judging or interpreting them. Despite his best efforts, he couldn't quite 'get' this core idea, so found himself repeatedly stumbling. 'It was a bit of a nightmare, to be honest,' said Drew. 'The trouble was, at work I'd spend the whole day judging and comparing, so the idea of simply noticing the presence of something goes against the whole grain of my character. So as soon as I noticed a feeling tone, the intellectual part of my mind would leap into action and begin judging the feelings. This part of me would then start firing off questions like: *Is that really pleasant? ... Are you sure? Now it feels a bit like nothing ... maybe a bit unpleasant ...*

Drew's experiences are not unusual. Judging and comparing are so central to our lives that it can be genuinely difficult to simply notice the presence of something – and then to stop right there with the actual noticing and not go a single step further. The idea that something *just is* can be a peculiarly difficult concept to accept. It feels so at odds with the Western 'rational' tradition that it can seem almost like a personal affront to many people. This is made worse because, superficially at least, registering can feel a bit like you *are* judging something, like you are *deciding* whether something is pleasant, unpleasant or neutral. So it can feel as if you are categorising it on an intellectual level, even when you are not. This difficulty is compounded by the very nature of the feeling tones themselves. They can appear very quickly, one after the other, particularly if you are feeling tired, stressed or rushed. If you spend time trying to judge an experience, rather than simply registering it, then the next feeling tone can arrive before you've finished evaluating the first, so the entire experience feels hurried, confusing and even exhausting.

'The whole thing was just so damn confusing!' said Drew. 'I'd spend ages tying myself in knots trying to decide whether I'd just registered a feeling tone or whether I'd judged it once again. Like I couldn't even just notice whether something was there or not.'

If you find yourself being drawn into such a swamp of overthinking, then as gently as you can, take a mental step back. Rather than trying to decide whether you have made a judgment rather than registering a feeling tone, simply notice what happens next. Each reaction leaves behind a little 'fingerprint': when you *register* a feeling tone, there is normally an immediate sense of simplicity, a feeling of moving on from the experience; by contrast, when you *judge* a feeling tone, there is a feeling of complexity and of loose ends that need tidying up – you might find yourself staying with the experience for longer, comparing it with similar ones from the past and becoming snarled up in your thoughts.

Amelie had similar difficulties to Drew: 'It's exactly what got me stuck, too. I found the concept of feeling tones very helpful at first. It was new to me and added an extra layer to the meditations. I'd got used to recognising my thoughts and feelings, so registering whether they were pleasant, unpleasant or neutral took the process further. But then questions started appearing in my mind. I found it really hard to stop at simply registering a feeling tone and then waiting for the next one to appear. My brain jumped in and started analysing: "Why was that pleasant, why does it make me feel calm?" "Why was that neutral?" "I used to like that, but not any more – why not?" "Why is that thought unpleasant?" "Why do I find it unpleasant when many others wouldn't?" So much thinking, thinking, thinking! When such thinking started, I'd be swept along by the thoughts and find myself miles away. Maybe back in my childhood, or wrapped up in my plans for next week or swamped with feelings of irritation. Sometimes it was all completely overwhelming.'

Such over-thinking is common. It's triggered when a thought kick-starts the 'conceptual' mind. This happens in two stages. Firstly, the intellectual mind wants to judge the experience, so it compares it with other experiences by drawing on memories of similar ones from the past. The mind then begins asking open-ended questions in a bid to pin down *why* the experience is the way that it is. Such questions as: why was I happy then and not now? Each little question keeps the mind churning over a little longer and leads to more over-thinking.

Noah had similar problems and became even more 'obsessed with getting it right': 'I found it very demoralising, like I couldn't succeed at it. I found that the feeling-tone meditations made my low moods worse. They brought back old memories and negative ideas about myself. I found it a challenge and got sucked into the idea that there was a right and wrong way to meditate, that it was quite tricky and easy to get wrong, and I became convinced that I *was* getting it wrong. I found myself constantly analysing my daily meditations and getting into a debate with myself about whether I'd "got it" yet. Then old circular thinking patterns started up.

I started obsessively asking myself, *What's wrong with me? I'm useless at this.*'

But Noah wasn't 'useless' and his experiences were not unusual. It is impossible to fail at meditation – and we mean this. Often, moments of apparent failure are quite the opposite. When you realise that your mind wanders and refuses to settle, when you judge rather than register the feeling tones, and more and more difficult feelings begin to appear, these are not moments of failure but moments of hope. They are moments of awareness, of mindfulness – moments when you are gaining a glimpse of your mind at work. And such glimpses will progressively give you the power to respond, rather than react.

Nevertheless, if you do find that powerful negative thoughts, feelings or emotions have begun to overwhelm you, gently remind yourself that you can pause the meditations for a while, or even let go of the formal practices for a day or two, and instead tune in to your feeling tones as you go about your normal everyday life. If this, too, should prove difficult or traumatic, you might even let go of the active labelling for a while and simply wait for a sufficiently clean and clear feeling tone to turn up.

Noah tried this and found it liberating: 'I stopped listening to the meditation tracks for a few days and decided to take a breather from the whole thing. Then a couple of days later, I was pouring some milk into a jug and noticed that it felt different. It was ... pleasant. I didn't need to consciously label it. I just knew it. After this, I was able to notice more pleasant and unpleasant moments without getting entangled in the process of looking too hard for them. It felt like I'd "cracked" it in some way – that I could do it if I didn't try too hard. That convinced me that the meditations were actually having a positive effect. It gave me the confidence to restart the practices.'

Some people can find the simplicity of feeling tones a little hard to grasp, fearing that they are missing some hidden element, nuance or complexity. Amelie found the following little exercise a useful way of clarifying things.

Grasping the simplicity of feeling tones

Imagine being thrown a ball. As soon as you catch it, you know if it is hard or soft; you don't have to think about it.

Can you sense the pleasantness or unpleasantness of a sensation, a sound or a thought or impulse in a similar way?

If you find yourself spending time thinking about the feeling tone, trying to work out what it is, or why it is as it is, see if it's possible to let go of the cognitive judgment and tune in to the immediacy of pleasant or unpleasant – just like the immediacy of the sense of a ball being hard or soft. And if there is nothing immediate to be felt – this is not a problem. Let the moment go and then wait for the next one to arrive.

Amelie found the idea of catching a ball and instantly knowing whether it was hard or soft especially useful. She appreciated the idea of a ball's softness being a sense rather than a thought. When she allowed the sense to be present, she found it easier to stop analysing the experience: 'It helped me enormously,' said Amelie. 'I wasn't consciously analysing my thinking. All I had to do was gently remind myself not to go into too much detail and then it became easier to avoid using complex logic. I just "got it" when I approached it in this way.'

An alternative is to do nothing at all: simply allow the mind to do what it does, seeing it clearly as 'thinking', and then noticing the feeling tone of the thought stream. After all, this is now in the foreground of your awareness. And if the thinking feels frustrating – then see if it's possible to notice the tonality of such frustration.

WANTING TO BE SURE

A little later, Amelie found herself agonising over whether she had truly identified a feeling tone or simply experienced the flicker of something else, such as a thought or a sensation. Feeling tones can be very subtle. And when they appear in the body, it's not always obvious at all. Sometimes they can feel more like a wave of sensation, a faint flicker or even a colour. So it's important to understand that you may find noticing them difficult, and this is perfectly OK, because it *can* be difficult. Understanding this can be a liberation in itself. When you let go of wanting to be sure, a space can open up where you can see what's around you, and one where you can begin to accept yourself.

Everyday Mindfulness Practice: An End-of-day Reflection on Feeling Tone

This practice extends your training by bringing attention to the feeling tone of what's been happening today.

1. Start by grounding yourself, noticing the contact of the body with whatever you are sitting or lying on, or anchoring your attention on the breath.

2. When you are ready, allow the events of today to come to your mind. As you recall each event, no matter how small or large, let it rest for a moment on the workbench of the mind, and notice its feeling tone – as it feels to you *now*. Is it pleasant, unpleasant or neutral?

3. If there seems to be no feeling tone to register, simply allow the next thing that happened to come to mind.

4. Notice if you are getting pulled into thinking *about* the experience, coming back as best you can to simply registering its tonality without judgment – pleasant, unpleasant or neutral – before moving to the next thing that happened. Perhaps imagine each event as if it were a pebble you are picking up on a beach, looking at it, then putting it down again.

5. To end the practice, come back to your anchor for a few moments.

As you move through Week Three, you may also notice that feeling tones can sometimes seem both pleasant and unpleasant. For Amelie, a slight headache co-existed with a pleasant sense of peace, then in the very next moment, both gave way to a pleasant tingling feeling. As Week Three unfolded, she found it easier to notice the very moment that a feeling tone arose and then to move on. Then, during the end-of-day practice, she said: 'I noticed less tendency to get drawn into stories. I just tasted the flavour of pleasant/unpleasant/neutral and that was enough.'

It can be particularly frustrating to repeatedly stumble at the same point in the meditation. Alex found it easy to sense the feeling tones in his body, but far more difficult to notice those associated with sound. It was especially tricky for him to isolate 'the very moment' the sound occurred and to sense the feeling tone at that very moment. He felt that something was wrong if he did not sense it immediately: 'I couldn't decide whether the sound was pleasant, unpleasant or neither. But this dithering was more of an afterthought, rather than an instantaneous reaction.'

Alex makes an important observation. Sometimes you only become aware of a feeling tone through its after-effects. For example, you may find yourself opening the refrigerator door or a cupboard in search of a snack and only then realise that you've experienced a number of 'neutral' feeling tones. In fact, you weren't looking for a snack at all, but rather, something to distract yourself away from boredom and restlessness. Sometimes, as meditation teacher John Peacock observes, we only know the feeling tone by its effects on our behaviour – what he calls the 'footprints it leaves in the sand'. When this happens, there's no need to criticise yourself. Instead, you can warmly congratulate yourself for having noticed. It is perfectly fine to notice the feeling tone 'down the road', instead of when it happens. In fact, sometimes we only become aware of feeling tones in this way.

If you should encounter difficulties similar to Alex's, try to persevere as best you can. See if it is possible to notice the tonality of first contact – the moment that you first become aware of a sound, a thought or a daydream. But also try to remember that it's OK if you are not aware of this first contact. You don't need to track back; instead, simply see if it's possible to become aware of the 'last contact' – that is, the sound or the thought or the part of the plan or daydream you were last aware of before you registered the feeling tone.

Some find it is helpful to explore *where in the body* a feeling tone is located. As you may have found with the examples in the box on page 108, it is often difficult to say *how* we know something is pleasant or unpleasant. It just is. The smile of a baby may simply be pleasurable without any detectable shift inside the body. If there is any sense of feeling tone in the body at all, it may be very subtle, such as a sense of 'opening' when experiencing pleasantness or a feeling of 'contracting' when experiencing unpleasantness. Such feelings may be found any-where in the body, but the stomach, chest, shoulders or throat are most common. If you find this difficult to do within your formal meditation practice, then simply look out for pleasant and unpleasant feeling tones in daily life. You may find they accompany the first taste of tea or coffee in the morning, your journey to work or to a friend's house or perhaps the sound of a heavy lorry bumping down the road outside. When they do appear, gently pause and note 'Ah, here is pleasant' or, 'Ah, here is unpleasant.' There's no further work required. Gradually, you may find that your mind and body naturally tune in to this dimension of experience.

BIAS TOWARDS NOTICING THE UNPLEASANT

For Kurt, feeling tones came through most strongly with things that were unpleasant: 'In the twenty-minute meditation, I began to see where my mind was going and noticed the feeling tone – and it was often not good. My mind always drifted towards things that were not pleasant – plans and things that I had to do and which I wasn't looking forward to doing. On one or two days of Week Three, I became fixated on the idea that I might lose my job.

My thoughts were going down a very dark rabbit hole. Again and again. The same hole! I could feel it in my body, too. Especially my stomach. Really churning, really unpleasant. Then I would recognise what was happening. I thought to myself, What's the point of worrying about this? I found it difficult to welcome distractions; I just wanted them to go away and let me get on with relaxing.'

It can sometimes feel as if the mind becomes fixated on the negative. When the mind becomes busy, it seems to draw you in, again and again, to the stories it creates. Sometimes it's possible to take a step back and see this happening, while on other occasions the stories are just too compelling. It can seem as if you're failing to get to grips with the practice. But rather than signs of failure, these are opportunities to deepen your practice. In such times, see if it's possible to watch the mind coming and going, so that the 'obstacle' becomes your mindfulness practice. You might try saying to yourself: 'Ah, here's thinking' or perhaps, 'Here's daydreaming' or 'planning' or 'distraction' or whatever feels most appropriate. Another approach is to say gently to yourself: 'This is what thinking feels like' or perhaps, 'This is what daydreaming feels like' or whatever feels most appropriate. Taking this approach opens up a space in which you can learn to welcome distractions, so that you can learn to register each one as pleasant, unpleasant or neutral. Then, when you notice yourself getting distracted by unpleasantness, or lost in thought, you can learn to notice its effect on your body, your feelings or impulses. You can learn to notice its tonalities and then continue with whatever you were doing.

Naming the feeling tone

There is something uniquely powerful about finding the words to describe how things feel. Naming a feeling tone brings it more keenly into awareness, acknowledges it and damps down the mind's tendency to rely on old habits and models. This, ultimately, gives you more choice.

Psychologist Matthew Lieberman showed that naming an emotion in the presence of negative pictures (for example, 'scared') reduces activity in the amygdala, widely seen as one of the most important centres of emotional reactivity in the brain.[4] Psychologist Michelle Craske and her colleagues[5] found that in people who were phobic of spiders, simply putting words on their experience ensured they showed less physiological reactivity to spiders and ultimately allowed them to get closer to the creatures. Psychologist David Creswell and others found that labelling emotional stimuli (photos of faces) engages more 'top-down' intentional activity in the prefrontal cortex, which dissolves automatic emotional responses, reducing their intensity and duration. People who are more mindful show this pattern more strongly; that is more top-down neural activation in the frontal part of the brain and greater decreases in amygdala reactivity. This pattern shows that mindfulness is associated with a more effective neural response to experiences.[6]

Taken together, this research shows that 'naming' the unpleasant is effective at reducing its impact, with mindfulness enhancing the effect and bringing with it greater peace and stability.

Sometimes thoughts can be so loud and insistent it is difficult to notice anything else. This is what Leila initially discovered, though later on, she found her thought stream gradually became quieter and less intrusive as such things as sensations, impulses and even sounds became more distinct. After a few days, she found herself 'going upstream' to catch the tonality of sounds, thoughts and sensations. So the feeling tones gave her something to explore, and, rather than solely focusing on thoughts and feelings themselves, she could go a little deeper. This was especially important in the mornings; she found it helpful to tune in to the feeling tone – to notice the pleasant and the unpleasant – as the first few moments of the day were unfolding. 'It allowed me to become aware of how I was approaching the day, and this was a new insight for me,' she said.

Sometimes Leila's thoughts would take her away completely into daydreaming or planning, but when she realised this, she found she could sense the feeling tone of the whole thought stream. Simply naming it as pleasant, unpleasant or neutral helped her to stand back from it, rather than getting swept along by it, or judging herself for having it.

This is how it feels sometimes. You may become aware of a 'general' feeling tone that is either an average of all the specific tones or it might mean that one sensory door is dominating the experience. If you find that one door is taking over – or that your thoughts have run away with themselves because they are distressing in some way – it may be helpful to ask yourself, 'What else is here, right now?' and then, after observing the result for a while, move on to asking which aspects of the body and mind are relatively neutral.

Toby said such a subtle approach reminded him of a 'dream-catcher'. Sensing tonality when something slightly pleasant or slightly unpleasant arises was like noticing the trembling of the dreamcatcher as the breeze blows through it. Toby then began to notice other times when the actual feeling tone did not match his expectations. For example, when he noticed an ache or pain in the body, he assumed that the feeling tone would always be unpleasant, but sometimes it was more neutral than he expected. These sorts of experiences started to have a more generalised effect on him.

'It's changed my perception completely,' he said. 'For example, I used to hate meetings. But recently, I've noticed that when I am about to attend a meeting the feeling tone is often more pleasant than I expected.' Toby then found that this change in attitude had significant knock-on effects: 'I realised that the meetings might not be that bad and this has affected the mood that I take with me into the meetings, which has been great for me and probably for others, too.'

This was similar to Frankie's experience. She said that her house is very quiet, 'ideal for meditation', as she put it, and quite pleasant. But this means that when there *are* sounds, they can be quite distracting. During her practice one morning, a motorbike went past and her attitude shifted from pleasant to unpleasant. Deep down she felt, 'It's a motorbike and motorbikes make unpleasant noises.' Interestingly, she noted that the sense of 'the motorbike making unpleasant noises' was part of her *general idea* of motorbikes, rather than her actual experience. It was the general idea that was unpleasant: the prediction. A distraction in one moment and her prediction about it, then her reaction to it, all unfolded in successive moments, with each having its own feeling tone, just like the moments of a horse running in Muybridge's pioneering photography (see page 30).

As you progress through this week, you may find yourself

developing sharper perception; a realisation that a moment doesn't have to be pleasant or unpleasant. It could be neither – just neutral – and this allows you to move on.

Kurt says: 'I'm better able to read my moods now, noticing the very moment an emotion begins to stir, and I can then choose how to respond. My partner called me for supper the other day and I hadn't quite finished what I was doing but I realised that I needed to go. As I went into the kitchen, I recognised that my thoughts and mood were still a little unpleasant. This is just the kind of situation where we'd normally argue over something. As I realised this, I got a flicker of another unpleasant feeling tone, but instead of rising to it and getting defensive, I found myself acknowledging it. I actually heard myself say inwardly: "Am I going to spread this feeling around, or can it stop now, with me?" That simple question led to a pause that allowed me to accept that although an uncomfortable moment had appeared, it need not escalate into a full-blown argument. So we ended up having a good meal. Such a little step but it's made a big difference. Things are much better between us.'

Drew had a similar experience. One night he was home early, so offered to read a bedtime story to his seven-year-old son: 'He's just at the age when he is reading some things by himself, but I thought he'd like me to do it like I used to do when he was younger.'

But his son was now old enough for sarcasm and was developing his own sense of humour, so he responded: 'Dad, you're too old for that story. And shouldn't you know it already?'

'Even though my son had a cheeky grin on his face, in the past I wouldn't have noticed it; just got annoyed and told him that he could just go and read the story all by himself. I'd then feel guilty for snapping at him. But on this occasion, I could sense the unpleasantness of my mood. It was a sort of contraction in the body, nowhere specific, but it was a very obvious unpleasant feeling tone. When I sensed this, it was enough to defuse the irritation and give me a moment's space to notice the pleasantness of his grin and make a better decision. It gave me a much more skilful way to handle the situation. I became genuinely interested in him and his reading instead of being focused on myself and my irritation. So instead of snapping at him, I asked him what book he was reading. As soon as I asked, his mood melted, too, we had a good chat about his favourite books and we took turns reading from Roald Dahl.'

Such transitions from unacknowledged feeling tones towards full awareness offer a taste of freedom. Naming your feeling tones, like naming your emotions, is extraordinarily powerful. *Unacknowledged* feeling tones trigger cascades of actual and imagined reactivity. *Acknowledged* feeling tones are different. Awareness of them offers a small gap, a moment that can change the seemingly inevitable cascade of emotion into a series of choices.

This way, wisdom lies

When we are distressed, what we remember from our past is coloured by our current state of mind. If we are feeling sad, hopeless or anxious, the memories we recall can acquire extra layers from the current emotion. Our memories are not set in stone. They are not like photographs or home movies – our recollection of the past is malleable; so not only does unhappiness lead to further unhappiness, stress to more stress and anxiety to further anxiety, but our memories are remade to further deepen such negativity.

It works like this: whenever we retrieve an item from memory, it is re-encoded, that is, affected by the context now, as well as the elements that were already in the memory. But this re-encoding means that what is put back into the memory store is different from what we took out. It could be better or worse – but it is not always the same. Research on eyewitness statements illustrates this well.[1] Participants were shown a video of a minor road-traffic accident. Some were asked: 'About how fast were the cars going when they hit?' Others were asked: 'About how fast were the cars going when they bumped?' And others '… when they smashed?'

The words used to describe the incident made a significant difference. Even though everyone had seen the same videos, if the word 'smashed' was used, then the witnesses recalled the cars going faster compared to those who had been 'primed' with the milder words. And a week later, if the word 'smashed' had been used, participants were more likely to see broken glass in their minds' eye, even though there was no broken glass in the video. So the language used at the time of recall affected the memory itself.

When we are bearing witness to our own lives, retrieving events and thinking about them, the same thing can happen. If you are angry or sad and then recall or think about something difficult, these feelings from the present moment can 'stick' to the memory and become integrated into it. And these altered memories also become integrated into the mental models used to build your simulation of the world.

This begs the question: why on earth should memory be so susceptible to such influences and become less accurate in the retelling? It's because the same feature has important benefits, too. It allows you to integrate what you have learned into a broader context. It allows you to link together discrete information and events to enhance your overall understanding. The very malleability of memory enhances understanding.

Imagine you are a teacher helping your students to prepare for an exam. You want them to remember what they have been taught earlier in the year, so you give them periodic tests and exercises. Not only do they get a chance to rehearse what they know, but this also helps them to put the older material into a wider context. Now, think back to a time when you told a good friend about a difficulty you were having in your life and they responded by deeply listening without judgment. You probably found that recalling the memory in such a loving environment altered it in a helpful way, perhaps putting it into a new context, allowing you to see new perspectives.

This is one reason why simply tuning into your feeling tones can be so therapeutic. Observing their rise and fall without judgment removes their sting and forestalls your entirely natural reactions to them. It is an act of kindness to yourself that allows thoughts, feelings, emotions, sensations and memories to be born into a wider and kinder space. This, in turn, enhances perspective and progressively dilutes your most troubling states of mind.

This way, wisdom lies.

CHAPTER EIGHT

Week Four: Restoring Balance

Don't get your hopes up, said the voice in Renata's mind. It was becoming a bit of a habit. Every time her spirits lifted, *that* voice from her childhood would pop into her mind and begin dampening her hopes for a better future. Ironically, she'd only begun to notice the voice after starting the Feeling Tone course. Before, it had simply been just another part of her mind's slightly depressing background chatter. Although it didn't always feel like it, the course was doing its job by teasing apart her troubles, bringing them out into the open, so that she could then begin to heal and, ultimately, start to live a more fulfilling life.

Although Renata had never suffered from clinical-level depression, much of her adult life had been marred by prolonged periods of generalised distress, angst and unhappiness. She could barely remember a time when she was truly happy, full of energy and genuinely enthusiastic about life. She had always found her inability to enjoy things a little unexpected. After all, she had many of the trappings of a reasonably good life, with none of the risk factors associated with depression (such as a major life trauma or a disturbed upbringing). In fact, Renata had what she describes as a thoroughly ordinary life with an average upbringing – an average family in an average town – and hadn't suffered any major tragedies at all. Her life and career trajectory were pretty good, too. She left home to go to college at eighteen, got a business-studies degree, came back home for a while, then settled down to a job in marketing for a small company a couple of hours' drive away from where she had grown up. She mostly enjoyed her job, and her career was going OK-ish.

'So what's gone wrong?' she often wondered.

Looking back, her slide into low-level depression had started so slowly that she'd barely noticed it. The current episode had begun the previous year, following a period of intense overwork. This meant she was often so tired that she had lost her zest for life, gradually turning down more and more invitations to go out with friends, instead watching more and more TV. Then her exercise classes fell by the wayside and she stopped cooking the wholesome foods she used to love. Although there was nothing obviously wrong, Renata's friends noticed her long, slow slide into unhappiness and stepped in to help. One friend recommended mindfulness, so she bought a book, then attended some sessions at a local yoga centre. These were helpful and so she decided to dive in and take this Feeling Tone course. At first, she found it fairly straightforward and felt like she was really getting to grips with the practices and the ideas behind them. The idea of choosing an anchor in Week One was particularly helpful to her, as her mild asthma could make her breathing a little unstable. The idea of 'Taking a Pause' in Week Two was useful as it reminded her that she had choices about where her mind went, and the invitation to have some gratitude or even wonder for her mind was a totally new idea for her. It gave her a fresh perspective, explained why her mind was always so frantic and busy and gave her a new way to work with it.

Then, in Week Three, Renata hit the buffers. Firstly, she found it very difficult to notice pleasant and unpleasant feeling tones. Then, when she did notice them, she would invariably start to analyse why she liked or disliked them, before getting lost in thought. She became increasingly frustrated with the meditations and then with herself for not being able to do them. Nevertheless, she persevered and began to value the invitation to view the 'distractions' as pieces of gym equipment that are good for training the mind. Hence the 'distractions' helped her gain a sense of what was troubling her. She gradually became aware of a theme that she had not noticed before – a half-hidden attitude that was affecting everything. Whenever she did manage to notice something she liked or disliked, she heard herself whispering to herself, 'You shouldn't like this' or, 'You shouldn't dislike that.' As the layers of her mind revealed themselves, she realised that whenever she sensed something as pleasant, the reaction was far more powerful. She found herself saying, 'This won't last long; don't get your hopes up.' After a while, she realised where the voice was coming from. It was from her past and had been sniping at her for decades without her realising it.

It had all begun when she was twelve. There was a maths challenge at school and the whole class had been entered. Renata was especially excited because she was good at maths and wanted to prove to the boys in her class that she was cleverer than them.

Her mum saw her excitement at breakfast and said: 'Don't get your hopes up too much. It's OK if you don't do as well as you want. Your dad and I won't mind.'

As the memories swirled around, Renata realised that her mum was clearly trying to protect her from disappointment if things did not go well. But it had simply made her feel bad about getting excited and dampened down the elation of her later success. This was a pattern in the family. When she was small, if she became excited when playing a game, her parents would invariably say, 'There'll be tears before bedtime.' Then, when she got older, the mantra became 'Don't get your hopes up.' Such phrases were trotted out whenever there was something to look forward to, such as a school prom, and especially when she was gearing up for something more challenging like an important exam or performing in the school play – and even on her first date. It even happened when she applied to university – one she really wanted to go to – and her mother cautioned: 'It's good to apply, but don't get your hopes up. There are other places.'

This discovery about the roots of her problems didn't make Renata dislike her mother. Quite the opposite. She realised that her mother had learned to distrust happiness because she had suffered so much hardship in her own life, and she was simply trying to protect her daughter from what she saw as the inevitable disappointments. And Renata understood that she had also formed the same habit. Rather than savouring moments of anticipation and happiness as they arose, she had learned to unwittingly dampen them down before she 'got her hopes up'. So now, whenever happiness beckoned, her mind would automatically swirl with such thoughts as, *This won't last, there's no point enjoying it, Pride comes before a fall* and especially, *All good things come to an end*. She remembered the fairy story in which the princess spun straw into gold. With a jolt she realised that she was doing the opposite: spinning gold into straw.

It is not just Renata who dampens life's high notes in this way. We all do. For unless we are truly mindful, we can flatten life's emotional peaks and fill its valleys with their rubble, reducing everything in the landscape to shades of grey. Not the shades of grey beloved of great photographers – where the nuances enhance the beauty – but the kind of all-pervading nothingness that strips life of all purpose and meaning. So when you dampen your hopes and dreams, you are not protecting yourself against failure, but setting yourself up for a lifetime of angst, uncertainty and loss.[1]

But there is an alternative to such dampening. It *is* possible to allow life's pleasures to nourish your spirit and begin to fully enjoy life once again. You can do it by paying attention to the rise and fall of your feeling tones in a way that was known to many ancient traditions but has long been forgotten in the West. You will begin by giving yourself permission – in a very special way – to enjoy life's pleasures. But this won't be quite enough. To truly restore balance, you also need to give yourself permission to dislike the unpleasant moments in your life without instinctively pushing them away. For unless you learn to allow the unpleasant vedana to arrive and to stay awhile – to genuinely feel it – you will not truly feel the pleasant moments in your life either. They are two sides of the same coin. Avoid one and you avoid them both. And you can learn to accept both by tuning in to your feeling tones, as you did last week, and then turning towards them and allowing them to linger and to dissolve, all by themselves. When you do so, you will find that your life begins rebalancing itself, all on its own.

Such radical acceptance is undoubtedly tricky, but you can do it by quietly saying to yourself a little phrase that helps you to *allow* the feeling tone to be just as it is, without trying to change it. This is the core practice for this week.

You will begin the practice, first by acknowledging the presence of the feeling tones as you meditate, before progressively doing the same in your daily life. Each time a pleasant moment arises, you can allow it to remain – and begin to truly feel it – by gently saying to yourself, 'It's OK to like this.' And when an unpleasant moment appears, you can gently say, 'It's OK not to like this.'

But first, a word of caution. When you say, 'It's OK ...', you are not saying that the *situation* that created the feeling is OK. Instead, you are saying that the feeling tone linked to that situation is OK and, indeed, natural. For example, if you have hurt your back, and it is painful, you are not saying that it is OK to be in pain. You are saying, 'It's OK *not to like* the pain.' Or if a memory of a past difficulty or trauma arises, you are not saying, 'It's OK that the trauma happened'; rather, you are saying that it's OK to find the memory unpleasant and that it is OK not to like it.

How can such a simple approach possibly work? Well, it is built on and sustained by almost 2,500 years of wisdom – the kind of wisdom that is present in all cultures and traditions but has been sidelined in the West and misunderstood by many others. So even if the precise mechanisms haven't quite been pinned down yet, modern psychology and neuroscience are beginning to understand the underlying reasons – and it is these that we will explore. First, though, you need to learn how to accept the rise and fall of your feeling tones, really connect with them, truly feel them. And then, you can begin to live once again.

Exercise is a particularly good way to explore feeling tones because the 'signal' is often stronger and more noticeable than it is during a sitting meditation. This is why this week, you will explore your feeling tones through mindful movement (mindful walking alternating with mindful stretches). Walking is a good way to practise because the mind is often daydreaming while we walk, so there are many chances to bring it back to the present moment – and to the body – and to observe the feeling tone. Similarly, with stretching, it is often when we are reaching for things that we realise we are rushing about a little faster than we need to, or overtaxing the body, so this can provide valuable 'gym equipment' for your daily practice.

Practices for Week Four

- **Mindful Walking** – either twenty minutes once a day (meditation 4.2) or ten minutes twice a day (meditation 4.1). This should be alternated with the Mindful Stretching practice (below) so that you do three days of each. Note in your journal how things go: any difficulties, delights and discoveries. Once you're familiar with the instructions, feel free to use the minimal instructions (Mi) version (4.4) or simply use the sound of bells as your timer. On at least one day this week, walk for thirty minutes, either using that specific version (meditation 4.3) or using any of the versions mentioned above.
- **Mindful Stretching Practice** – on alternate days. There is one meditation (4.5) lasting twenty minutes to guide you until you are familiar with the sequence. After this, feel free to let go of the guidance.
- **Ten-finger Gratitude Exercise** – once a day (meditation

4.6). After a few days, move on to the minimal instructions (Mi) version (4.7) or perhaps with no instructions at all.

- **Everyday Mindfulness Practice: Appreciation.** Each day, look out for any small moment when you notice something *pleasant*. You can follow the audio guidance (4.8) for the first few days before practising it without.

We have added a bonus meditation this week to use for those who find it hard to sleep (meditation 4.9).

All meditations for this week can be found at littlebrown.co.uk/deeper-mindfulness/week-4

The meditations can also be found on the authors' website at franticworld.com/ deeper-mindfulness

The core practices this week are not the exercises themselves but how you respond to the feeling tones as you carry out the movements. During mindful movement, whether walking or stretching, if you notice a *pleasant* feeling tone, gently say silently to yourself, 'It's OK to like this.' The aim is to help you appreciate the moment *as it is*, without dampening or trying to deepen or prolong it. If you find an *unpleasant* feeling tone, gently say silently to yourself, 'It's OK not to like this' and see if it's possible to hold the sense of unpleasantness in a wider and more spacious awareness for a moment.

Some people have strong reactions to mindful movement, so you may find yourself reacting to even the thought of it, the liking or disliking of it, or perhaps just finding it boring. See if it's possible to move in close to such reactions and pay attention to any moment-by-moment thoughts, feelings and impulses and also to what happens next. Tune in to the very moment you notice whether the reaction is pleasant or not, and see if you can follow up by allowing it to be just as it is by gently saying inwardly, 'It's OK to like this' or, 'It's OK not to like this.'

Mindful Walking

In this practice, we take walking – a very ordinary activity – and do it in a way that helps train the mind and body to focus attention in the face of the small distractions that often occur when we're moving. The aim is to learn to tune in to feeling tone when it occurs, and to cultivate a sense of allowing it to be just as you find it.

Preparation

1. Begin by finding a place where you can walk up and down for a few paces, inside or outside – a place where you won't be disturbed or overlooked. The length of your path is not important – it might be as short as a yoga mat, or as long as ten paces.

2. Start by standing with your feet parallel to one another, about hip-width apart. If the ground or floor is suitable, you could remove your shoes and socks so that you can sense it more clearly under your feet. Allow your arms to hang loosely by your sides or hold your hands together

in front or behind your body, looking softly slightly down-wards or straight ahead.

Walking

3. Bring the focus of your awareness to the bottom of your feet, noticing the physical sensations of the contact that both feet make with the floor or the ground.

4. When you are ready, begin to walk, taking small, nat-ural steps and noticing as each foot makes contact with the ground, experiencing the weight of the body shifting as each foot comes off the ground, lifts and moves forwards.

5. Continue to walk with full awareness from one end of your path to the other.

6. When you come to the end of your path, turn slowly around, appreciating the pattern of movements through which the body changes direction, and then, when you are facing back along your path, pause for a moment and when you're ready, walk back.

Registering feeling tone …

7. If you notice that the mind has wandered away from the sensations in the feet, pause, acknowledging where the mind had gone, and register its feeling tone – pleasant, unpleasant or neutral.

... and allowing it to be as it is

8. And at any point, if you find your experience feels pleasant, say silently to yourself, 'It's OK to like this.'

    If you find your experience unpleasant, acknowledge this, too, by saying to yourself, 'It's OK not to like this.'

    Then, when you're ready, escort the focus of your attention back to the feet. Remember not to try too hard; if it's too difficult to sense the feeling tone immediately, let it go and wait for something else to come.

9. If the mind is very restless, it may be helpful to pause for a moment mid-path, and just stand, feet hip-width apart, noticing the weather pattern in the mind and the feeling tone of it, whether it's pleasant or unpleasant or neutral. If you choose, you could also register the feeling tone in body and mind whenever you pause at the end of your path.

10. Choose whatever pace feels to you most helpful during this time of mindful walking: sometimes walking slowly, sometimes walking at a more usual pace. If you wish, you may like to expand your attention during the practice, from the narrow focus on your feet to your legs and hips, and then, later, in your own time, to the whole body and what's around you as you move.

Ending

11. Continue this practice in silence by yourself, until the bells signal that it's time to end. And, as you bring this

practice to a close, form an intention to bring the same quality of awareness that you've been cultivating in this meditation to your normal, everyday experiences of walking. You do not have to walk very slowly as you move around in your day. Even slowing down just a little bit as you move from one thing to another may allow you to walk upright, rather than leaning forwards into the next moment, and, in this way, it can change your whole day.

Mindful Stretching

The intention of this meditation is to cultivate awareness of the body in movement, to tune in to the feeling tone (pleasantness or unpleasantness) and, especially, to learn to allow it to be as it is.

Remember that it's important to be gentle with yourself as you do these stretches. Look after yourself during the movement and let the wisdom of your body decide what is OK for you: how far to go with any stretch and how long to hold it. If you have any physical problems at the moment, do consult your physician or physical therapist before embarking on even these simple stretches. If you are not sure if you can manage a stretch, you could remain still, cultivating awareness of the body just as it is, whether at rest or in movement.

If any movement feels too intense, there's always the option of simply imagining doing it, or moving only very slightly at any time or coming out of the posture and moving back, no matter what the guidance on the track is inviting you to do. It's also fine to do the practice sitting down. This is because it isn't the particular movement you're doing that is most important but the awareness you bring to it.

Pause between each posture to tune in to the after-effects of the stretch – the sensations and the feeling tone of sensations – breathing freely and easily, in whatever way your body wants to, as you stretch and when you are between stretches.

Allowing

At each point in the practice, as you become aware of any unpleasant sensations or dislike, acknowledge this, allowing it, by saying inwardly, 'It's OK not to like this.' And as you become aware of any sensation that feels pleasant, allow this as well, saying inwardly, 'It's OK to like this.'

The suggested sequence is as follows:

- Start by choosing whether to stand or sit.
- Stretch the hands above the head, with the palms facing each other.
- Stretch up first with one hand and then the other, as if picking fruit.
- With the feet a little further apart, with your hands on your hips for support, the body makes a curve over to the left side; then moving to do the same on the other side.

At this point, if you've been standing, you could move to sit on a chair, stool or cushion for the remainder of the stretching practice.

• When you are settled, move the shoulders up, back, down and forwards, staying in each position long enough to register the sensations and their feeling tone. Then roll the shoulders very slowly, first in one direction and then the other, picking up the changing sensations, the feeling tones that they create, and allowing them to be as they are.

Ending

And for the last few moments of the practice, become aware of the tonality of mindfulness itself. Remembering that awareness of the body is available to you at any moment of your day, allowing you to feel grounded, balanced and have a sense of accepting yourself just as you are.

IS IT *REALLY* OK TO DISLIKE THIS?

Jonathan had particular difficulties with Week Four. He felt that saying, 'It's OK not to like this' was a sign of ungratefulness and, like Renata (earlier in the chapter), it arose from his childhood.

Jonathan's parents were strongly religious and believed that expressing dissatisfaction was a rejection of God's providence. Their belief was that you must always be thankful – even while suffering. 'My parents were lovely people of faith, but they had this "thing" about God's providence and sin,' said Jonathan. 'Disliking something – anything, really – meant that you did not have enough faith and were consequently a bad person. God had laid out a path for us. Times of suffering are tests of faith; lessons that we should learn from; lessons to keep us on the straight and narrow path. Any grumbling, or anything that even hinted at ungratefulness, was a sin. I don't share their faith, well not much of it, but I'd still soaked up these attitudes without realising it.'

In practice, even disliking something as mundane as a wet winter's day made him feel ungrateful, which would trigger negative repetitive thought patterns, leaving him feeling anxious and fearful. The practices in Week Four seemed to compound this problem because even saying to himself 'It's OK not to like this' flew against his decades of conditioning. But his problems ran even deeper than this. Jonathan had been taught not only to not *express* dissatisfaction, but also not to *feel* it either. So his sense of 'not complaining' had morphed into a vicious restriction on his ability to feel – and to know – what is true. This can be particularly true for those who have felt chronically vulnerable in the past or been attacked, abused or traumatised by their history.

Over many years, both Renata and Jonathan had learned to suppress their most basic feelings. If they felt unpleasant feelings of dislike, frustration or anger, they would suppress them. And if they felt the pleasant feelings of happiness beginning to emerge, they would suppress those, too. Both of them ended up feeling ever worse: ashamed if they felt positive about some things; ungrateful if they didn't like others; annoyed when overwhelmed; guilty if they got angry.[2] For these reasons and more, it is important to stress, once again, that when you say 'It's OK ...', you are not referring to the pleasant or toxic situations themselves but to your natural feelings of liking or disliking them. Acceptance of your feeling tones is key here; positive, negative or neutral. Feeling tones should be felt, and when they are, they will have successfully delivered their message, so the chances are they will then quietly depart, leaving you feeling far more peaceful and content with the ensuing moments.

Pawla encountered problems with the first three weeks of the course, but these difficulties began dissipating during Week Four, albeit only after a difficult first few days: 'I really struggled. I'm a very physical person. I like things to be solid and grounded. I hate all of this "airy-fairy" stuff about the mind creating simulations of the world rather than sensing it directly. It seemed to be saying that the real world is not real, that it's some kind of dream or hallucination. Of course it's all real – although I'm open to the idea that it might not be real in quite the way that we think it is.'

Despite her initial reservations about how the mind constructs a picture of the world, Pawla persisted with the course for one simple reason: with her own eyes she could see just how much her classmates were benefiting from it. She also heeded the advice of her teacher when she pointed out that 'belief' in mindfulness and feeling tones are not important in themselves. The meditations are not like incantations or prayers. And they are not magic. Instead, they are practices that begin to make changes as you gently persist with them and put the effort in. This is why they are called 'practices'.

As her meditation teacher said: 'You don't need to know where feeling tones come from. You don't need to change them or make them go away. You only need to "turn on the light" to see them more clearly, and be more kindly towards them and yourself when they appear. And then you can see what happens; they may dissolve of their own accord – even the most powerful and distressing ones.'

Pawla finally 'got it' during one of her Mindful Stretching practices: 'I'd had a bit of a headache earlier in the day and felt tired. After I'd been stretching for a few minutes, I noticed that the feeling tone of my whole body was unpleasant. I realised that I still had the headache, and this was the source of the unpleasantness. Rather than just putting up with it, I thought, *This sensation is unpleasant*. And then, *It's OK not to like it*. What happened next was amazing. The headache just disappeared. It completely went. A few minutes later, I noticed another pain in my head, so I acknowledged it again: *It's OK not to like this sensation*. Once again, it dissolved and was replaced by a slight sense of ache and tingling where the pain had been. It was nowhere near as unpleasant.'

Pawla's experiences are an elegant illustration of how the mind's cache works in practice, and how simply acknowledging the presence of a feeling tone clears out the old and distressing information and refreshes it with the new. In Pawla's case, the pain of her headache had left a sensory 'echo' in her mental cache. The cache then replayed this echo back to her on an endless loop. Although the pain of the headache varied from moment to moment, the cache had stored only a snapshot of the most intense moment (the 'peak pain') because this was the most salient and important one; the one that her mind believed she needed to be reminded of (see diagram opposite). This painful echo from her immediate past ricocheted into the present and then on to her future. She ended up reacting to a pain that no longer existed with quite the same intensity that it had just a few minutes previously. Saying 'It's OK not to like this' was enough to let go of that echo. And this allowed Pawla to feel what was truly happening in the present moment, as it happened – which was quite different to what she expected.

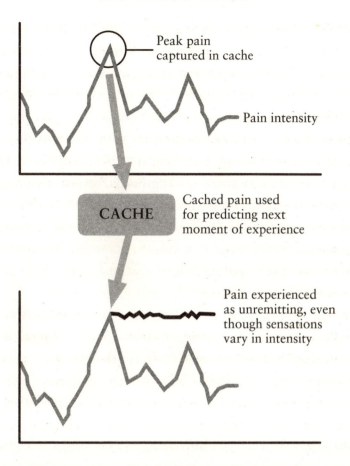

Peak pain
captured in cache

Pain intensity

CACHE

Cached pain used
for predicting next
moment of experience

Pain experienced
as unremitting, even
though sensations
vary in intensity

How 'peak pain' can ricochet into the present and future.

'If the headache had persisted, I would've gone and taken a painkiller. I'm not into bearing pain for its own sake. As it happens, later that same day, I experimented with other little aches and pains and found the same thing. And also at night. Often, I cannot sleep because of some arthritic pain that I get these days. I find myself tossing and turning, trying and failing to get comfortable. I tried saying to myself: "This is unpleasant; it's OK not to like it", and it was amazing. What's really strange is how in each case I had been sure that the pain was still there, but when I looked into it, it wasn't actually there in any such intensity. So I really was experiencing an echo of a previous pain. The actual pain was far less than I thought. And after that, sleep came much more easily.'

Although Pawla's pain did dissipate when she paid attention to it, this doesn't mean it wasn't real, that she wasn't feeling it or that she was imagining it or 'making it up'. And the same applies to your own pain. However, its origins are different to what you may have believed and its intensity will vary from moment to moment far more than you expect. Importantly, this means that you can learn to let go of much of your suffering.

In Pawla's case, why did she not notice that her pain was waxing and waning all by itself? And why did she not notice that sometimes it was completely absent? Well, like most of us, she simply didn't want to turn towards the sensations of pain.[3] She feared that it would be too intense. Instead, she wanted to turn away from it, push it away, pretend that it didn't exist. So all she was aware of was the painful echo stored in her mental cache rather than the real-time data from her senses. The simple act of paying attention to her feeling tones had reconnected her to the quiet moments that lie between even the most intense of sensations. And in such quiet moments, we can often find a measure of peace from whatever is troubling us.[4]

Transforming pain during childbirth

Learning to observe intense pain can, paradoxically, transform the experience for the better. Even during the most intense episodes of pain, you can often find periods of relative peace. A good example is provided by the pioneering work of Nancy Bardacke at the Osher Center for Integrative Medicine, University of California, San Francisco (UCSF). She developed the Mindfulness-based Childbirth and Parenting (MBCP) course to help parents better cope with pregnancy, birth and childcare. In her book *Mindful Birthing*,[5] she teaches expectant parents how best to manage the pain of childbirth. She uses blocks of ice, held in the hand, to prepare parents for pain that feels difficult, but which is not, in itself, dangerous. This helps them understand that it is common to miss the moments between contractions when there is no pain. This is understandable if the most intense sensations are stored in the mental cache, with unpleasant feeling tones contributing to the predictions of intense pain. MBCP has been shown to ease the process of childbirth and parenting, reduce pregnancy-related anxiety and depression and help parents to make more informed choices about the birth itself.[6]

Alex also hit a crisis point in Week Four – and he picked a path through his difficulties with the help of his mindfulness teacher. He did this by treating his mental anguish in the same way that Pawla responded to her physical pain. He emptied his mental cache of its recurring mental pain by consciously accepting the unpleasantness of his distress.

His crisis began with an email. Late one evening, he was sorting out plans for a 'meet-up' for a caravan club he belonged to. It was a group of friends who had met many years previously on a caravan site and decided to meet again. Now their children had all grown up and left home, but the old team got together at least once each summer. It was always a lovely highlight of the year. But a few years previously, the group had fractured following an argument with a couple who accused the others of leaving them off an invite. This soured the atmosphere, with the couple eventually leaving the group, saying that they didn't want to receive any more messages. Everyone respected their wishes until Alex, quite by mistake, included them again. He was sending out a quick email to everyone about this year's meet-up and, after he'd sent it, he realised with horror that he'd used an old list, and the couple's names were on it. 'Ah, well,' he thought. 'They might have changed and want to get back in touch.'

Two minutes later, an email arrived: 'Why have you emailed us? Don't you even check before you send something out? TAKE US OFF THIS LIST!'

Alex was upset. He felt bad about his mistake, and embarrassed, too, as the person had copied the angry message to everyone. His mood was vulnerable at the best of times, but this event made him feel terrible. He decided to practise his mindful walking.

As he walked, his mind soon wandered off and he began brooding about the evening's events, thinking he ought to 'give up the club'.

What's the point? he thought. *I'm always making mistakes. Always letting people down.*

He felt his distress mounting. *What's the point of my mindfulness practice? It never works when I need it most. How can I accept this awful situation? Why should I accept it?*

He once again tried focusing on his stream of thoughts, but they were relentlessly unpleasant. Then he remembered the advice of his mindfulness teacher about 'turning on the light' by inwardly naming the feeling tone 'unpleasant', then adding, 'It's OK not to like this.'

The whole distressing bundle of negativity dissolved.

'It was a total surprise,' he said. 'I continued to walk up and down, but five minutes later the whole stupid email exchange popped into my mind again. This time, though, a different emotion appeared. I wasn't upset with myself but very angry with the other couple. I was furious. Then my thoughts began swirling around and I started brooding over it all. After a couple more minutes getting angry and upset, I remembered to pay attention to how it felt. How my feeling tones actually *felt*. It wasn't easy to shift from brooding to focusing on feeling tone, but I did manage it. I said to myself, "Ah, this is unpleasant, too. It's OK not to like it" – and the same thing happened; it dissolved.

'Something like this would normally have continued for days, maybe even weeks,' said Alex. 'I would have ended up in a horrible state of mind. A deep, dark, mood that simply would not lift, no matter how much I argued against it. I would have argued logically with myself. I would have pointed out that I was overreacting, being overly sensitive, that it was the other couple that was causing the problem and that it was time for me to push back against them. Then I would have begun to hate them, then the caravan club and I would eventually have begun hating myself for being full of hate. It would have gone on like this day after day. But this time it didn't. I stopped the downward spiral before it had begun to run out of control.

'To recognise the mood, to see its feeling tone, then to recognise the distress it was causing me, and then to watch it dissolve – just by saying to myself, "It's OK not to like this" – was a revelation. It felt like a miracle.'

Tess found the mindful walking was a challenge for a very

different reason. Try as she might, every time she tried to focus on the sensations of walking, her mind would race off. It would do almost anything but focus on the meditation at hand. Most often, she'd start having what she believed were 'inappropriate thoughts and fantasies' about her friend's husband – and occasionally about the friend herself.

'My problem is, quite simply, I have a staid and "inattentive" husband who I now struggle to relate to. That's the downside. The upside is we have a very comfortable life together with three happy and healthy kids. Normally, I can shoo away the inappropriate thoughts and fantasies, but during the walking meditation they came to dominate. It seems wrong to say, "It's OK to like this" because, well, the thoughts are wrong.'

All of us, at least occasionally, have thoughts, feelings and impulses that we are ashamed of and would be horrified if other people knew about them.[7] And yet, it is perfectly normal to have them. You can do little about the spontaneous thoughts, images and impulses that appear in your mind. But you can do something about what happens next – you can choose how you relate to them and certainly whether you act on them or not. Ethics are about behaviour, not the contents of your mind. If you conclude that 'I'm a bad person' or 'I am going crazy' or 'I am dangerous' when you have such thoughts, then this will only make you feel worse, deepening your more vulnerable moods; and it is also more likely that the thoughts will return.

Deep down, Tess knew all this but still felt bad about her fantasies. They would always become particularly prominent as she did the walking meditation but, despite this, she managed to continue with the movement, bringing as much mindfulness as she could to them. Gradually, millimetre by millimetre, she started to see them for what they were – mental events, pleasant, unpleasant or neutral. As she walked back and forth along her hallway, she managed to watch as they came and went. She heeded the advice of her teacher and paid attention to how each 'inappropriate' thought triggered powerfully pleasant feeling tones, and to how her reaction to them – feeling guilty and ashamed – triggered waves of unpleasant feeling tones.

'I remembered something that the teacher had said: mindfulness of feeling tone has a kind of "guardian-angel" function. It's about "clear seeing" – including seeing where something might lead. It helped me to step back early enough to see the bigger picture. I began to see the distinction between acknowledging the thoughts and impulses on the one hand and feeding and indulging them on the other. Thinking is one thing but acting on those thoughts is another – and quite often they are a million miles apart.'

Fundamental to such 'clear seeing' is directly knowing the difference between fantasy and reality, so that you can then act wisely. Thoughts, images and impulses such as those Tess experienced may seem to be undermining your deepest values – but they are not. They are simply thoughts, images and impulses. Nothing more. They are not real. They are not commands that must be obeyed. Nor are they *you* – because you are not your thoughts. Simply noting their presence without judgment allows them to dissolve in their own time. And if you feel particularly vulnerable, and your behaviour in the past has caused you problems, such an approach grants you the time to distance yourself from risk. Those struggling with addictions and risky behaviour may find it particularly helpful. It helps you to anticipate the moments of greatest danger, such as those times when you are tired, hungry, lonely or angry. There is something about such times that cultivates a sense of entitlement which, in turn, reduces our ability to choose wisely. We all have weaknesses and addictions, great or small, and knowing our personal vulnerabilities is priceless. For example, if you have had problems with gambling, this approach might mean for you not walking past a betting shop or blocking certain websites; if you have had difficulties with alcohol, it might entail not walking past a particular bar. Such 'mindful avoidance' can be a good strategy.[8]

The opposite strategy – and one that's guaranteed to lead to great distress – is 'mindless avoidance'. And it's an easy trap to fall into. Earlier in the chapter we heard about Jonathan's inability to accept life's positive experiences. This had its roots in his upbringing, which subconsciously compelled him to avoid being seen as ungrateful by squashing his ability to express dislike for anything. But it had also undermined his ability to appreciate the positive things in life. As you will recall, being able to appreciate the pleasant things in life is the flipside of learning to approach the negative skilfully. Avoid one and you avoid both.

But there is also another reason why we don't experience the pleasant. We are just too busy. Our minds are always preoccupied with the future. We're always on our way to somewhere else, leaning forwards into the next moment; and, quite often, our minds have arrived at our destination before we've even set off. We rarely notice the present moment unfolding right here and now. This means that the 'lesser' things pass us by simply because we are not consciously present to notice and appreciate them. And this is compounded by the mind's subtle biases.[9] To reveal these, meditation teacher Martine Bachelor asks her students to imagine a scale of unpleasantness to pleasantness of -10 to +10. It turns out, most of us are highly sensitive to the negative. We're good at noticing unpleasantness of -1, but on average, it takes a pleasantness score of +5 to get our attention: the 'small' pleasant moments repeatedly pass us by. It may take time to shift the balance of a lifetime but thankfully, you can do so using the practices below. And you can make a start right now.

Ten-finger Gratitude Exercise

This is a short daily practice to help you tune in to and appreciate the 'small' pleasant moments of your life.

1. Take time to settle and ground yourself, sitting or lying down. At a certain point, allow your attention to settle on your breath, and then, when you're ready, expand your attention to the body as a whole, sitting or lying.

2. Allow yourself to look back over the last twenty-four hours, or over the period since you last practised in this way and bring to mind ten things you are grateful for. Count them on your fingers, bringing into awareness the ordinary things in the day.

3. See if you can carry on until you've got to ten, even when it gets harder after four or five. At this point, intentionally bring into awareness the tiny, often unnoticed, ordinary things of the day – like the water in a tap, the washing, the drying, the first mouthful of a meal, the first sip of a hot drink, the smile of a passer-by, a breeze moving the trees or the colour of a wall. There may be other things too – big or small – all waiting to be noticed.

4. Then, when you are ready, come back to the breath, perhaps completing the ten-finger exercise by appreciating the life-giving nourishment of each breath — this breath, and this breath, following one after the other (meditations 4.6 and 4.7).

Everyday Mindfulness Practice: Appreciation

Each day, look out for any small moment when you notice something pleasant. It doesn't have to be anything big or important. But when you notice it, see if you can take a pause, inwardly, for a moment. Notice in that very moment: what body sensations are here? Tune in to the body as it stands or sits or moves, allowing it to be as it is, perhaps saying inwardly, 'It's OK to like this.' (Try using meditation 4.8: Appreciation for a couple of days to get you started.)

For Renata, paying such close attention to what she appreciated – so difficult in the beginning – became easier with practice.

'Ten things?' she said. 'That sounded like an awful lot at first! That's about one or two things happening every couple of hours – even at work ... Not easy at all.

'I made a point of starting this one after a lovely meal on Friday evening and several hours after I'd returned from work. I thought it would be a nightmare, but once I decided to focus on the small but obvious things, it became a lot easier. My evening meal had two pleasant elements – and a glass of wine afterwards made it three. I soon got to seven positive things and then began to struggle but I did get to ten eventually.'

Renata found it made her think clearly about the day's events – its upsides and downsides. And she also noticed it had a positive effect on the next day as well. By the middle of the week, she'd begun to notice small, pleasant features of her day in time to appreciate them as they were actually happening. She found that using her fingers to keep track helped, too. She found herself touching her fingers together lightly as a sign to herself: 'This is a moment I am appreciating' – a moment of awareness. She realised that the movement practice and gratitude went together for her. She said she had previously 'not been aware of how my feet work!' She found herself really grateful for the simplicity of walking and stretching.

Like Renata, Jonathan really struggled at first: 'You would think that coming from a family that insists on being grateful for everything would make it easy for me, but . . . no.' By the middle of the week, however, he'd realised that the ten things did not have to be big and obvious events. Then he noticed something quite subtle. His emotional range began to expand. Like Renata, he was beginning to experience the pleasant – and unpleasant – things as they happened.

'It was like someone switched on the light at the end of a concert. You know, you can suddenly see all the smiling faces, hear the thunderous applause falling away into silence, experience the tingles of excitement spreading across your skin – and, of course, you also notice that there's lots of litter strewn across the floor and the bits of the walls that need painting. But, but, but . . . it is all real. And it is all lovely and exciting, and also dark and a bit grubby. I think it might be called "being alive".

'That is how it all felt to me. After years of suppressing the unpleasant and the pleasant ... suddenly, I could feel alive again.'

As the week progressed, Jonathan's mind began to naturally tune in to the little things: one day he was walking for ten minutes and noticed he was enjoying the sensations of his feet on the cool floor, then mentally noting, *Ah, pleasant*. Then, *It's OK to like this*. Then he noticed the fresh air brushing against his face. *Pleasant* – and, *It's OK to enjoy this*. Gradually, he found that this new attitude of 'allowing' was becoming established; it was taking less effort. He felt that it was also OK to slow down – to get into his body and his feet, to be there for this moment, too. He had started to notice the +1s and the +2s – 'This sandwich tastes good; my shoes feel comfortable; I've not got that headache today; that water was cool to drink.' He found so many little things to be grateful for: moments of ease and relaxing in the morning, cool temperatures, conversations with his partner, a delicious Sunday lunch, an afternoon nap, that first sip of afternoon tea, reading a novel, watching the TV, sunset over the hills, the first glimpse of the evening stars, watching his favourite soccer team win on TV ... And if ever he didn't get to ten fingers, he simply focused on the next few breaths – this breath, and this one, and this one – with a deepening sense of gratitude and even awe as he saw again how nourishing and life giving each breath truly is.

CHAPTER NINE

Week Five: Feeling Tone on the Fringes of Consciousness

In the atmospheric start to the trilogy *His Dark Materials*,[1] author Philip Pullman describes a scene in which a young girl moves slowly through the empty, gloomy hall of an ancient college, the tables laid ready for guests.

> 'Lyra reached the dais and looked back at the open kitchen door and, seeing no one, stepped up beside the high table. The places here were laid with gold, not silver, and the fourteen seats were not oak benches but mahogany chairs with velvet cushions.
>
> Lyra stopped beside the Master's chair and flicked the biggest glass gently with a fingernail. The sound rang clearly through the Hall.'

Pullman is fascinated by modern physics and uses some of its principles to explore literary ideas. He asks in one essay, what is the fundamental particle of a story – the smallest element that it can be broken down into?[2] You might think that stories are made from words, he says – but most of us started out as children with picture books. Surely language is essential at some point? Until you realise that you can tell stories through ballet, mime or music.

Pullman writes: 'I think stories are made from events, and that the fundamental particles of story are the smallest events we can find.'[3] He uses the example of pouring milk into a cup – or poison into someone's glass. In *Northern Lights*, it's Lyra's actions, the things she does, such as 'reached the dais . . .', 'looked back . . .', 'stepped up . . .', 'flicked the biggest glass . . .' Why do such events count as fundamental particles? It's because each event, each little action, conjures up a mental picture, along with its accompanying sounds, smells, tastes, thoughts, feelings, emotions and even sensations. They encapsulate a moment in time; a single picture in a photo burst. And when each particle is followed by another, and another, it conjures up a stream of consciousness that whisks us away into a world where the storyteller is king.

There is a reason why such 'story particles' are so powerful (and why Pullman is such a good storyteller): they tap into the mind at a fundamental level. When Pullman talks about actions being the 'particle of a story', the same is also true for the mind. Actions are also the fundamental particles of consciousness – each action, a single frame in a series of mental models; the photo burst that can so easily cascade out of control.

We understand the world through action, and the objects we interact with become part of our 'extended mind'. Allow us to explain this new and exciting idea. You may find the following pages a little counterintuitive in places, but they will offer you a radically new insight that promises to take your practice to a wholly different level. They are based on the latest advances in neuroscience, largely unknown until recently; and, paradoxically, many of the ideas bear a striking resemblance to early Buddhist and Ancient Greek philosophy.

The story begins with the way we think and make sense of the world. Psychologist Steve Tipper and his team have spent many years investigating consciousness and attention and discovered startling parallels with Philip Pullman's ideas. It turns out that we don't understand the world by logically thinking about it, but instead build up a picture by physically interacting with it. Even at the most basic level, we only perceive and understand objects as our minds and bodies try to work out what we can do with them.[4] Merely viewing an object, such as a cup, activates the brain regions needed to grasp it, even if there is no intention to do so, and no action is subsequently taken.[5] Simply recognising a cup – understanding what it is and what it can be used for – is carried out by the mind and body running through a simulation of its uses.[6] As far as the mind is concerned, an object contains a lot of information about itself. So in an odd kind of way, the brain outsources a bit of its memory to the object, so it becomes part of a greater, or extended mind. And understanding its uses becomes embedded, or implicit, in the object – so you *just know* how to use it without having to think about it.

The same is true for everything that you come across. If you see the word 'hammer' the area of the brain needed to use a hammer is activated and again you *just know* how to use it and what it can be used for.[7] If you are a driver and hear the word 'car', you simulate driving it in both mind and body without any conscious thought at all. It all happens subconsciously and automatically. And such 'particles of action' are strung together, frame by frame, to create streams of consciousness that whisk you away to a land where your simulation reigns supreme.

In practice, this means that whenever you see or perceive anything, there is also an automatic 'readiness to act' just below the threshold of awareness. Rather than simply being a downstream consequence of perception, imagined actions and responses are critically involved in understanding the world. The brain processes concerned with *perceiving* action and *performing* the same action are similar. Studies bear this out. For example, showing that if you are asked to judge the weight of an object lifted by somebody else, your own brain's motor and somatosensory system is activated (the same system that would have been activated had you lifted the object yourself).[8] So your body automatically prepares for action. To investigate these ideas, Steve Tipper and colleagues carried out an experiment in which participants were shown a short video of a hand picking up a coffee mug, while their brain activity was recorded to see if a critical part of the brain (one known to change when carrying out an action) is also affected when simply observing someone else performing an action.[9] The experiment showed that the characteristic change in the brain took place, as if the volunteer had picked up the mug themselves.[10] Witnessing an action had primed the participants' bodies to react in the same way, and the brain and body systems central to perception were shown to be the same as those central to action.

In practice, this means that the state of your body is central to interpreting and understanding the world.[11] This also extends to empathy, compassion and understanding other people in general, too, because there are specialised 'mirror neurons' in the brain that simulate the actions of others. So if you see someone stub their toe on a chair leg, you wince and feel a measure of their pain. If you see someone laugh, cry or become angry, you feel their emotion by acting it out in your mind and body. You sense the actions of others as if you, yourself, were carrying them out.[12] This is central to many addictions, too. It's why an alcoholic might be at risk of relapsing at the mere sight of a bottle of wine – or a cocaine addict at the sight of white powder. It also explains why waves of positive or negative sentiment can sweep through society; and why propaganda (and social media networks) are so powerful.

This brings us to the heart of the issue: your mind carries out much of this activity below the surface of awareness without any conscious input or control at all. This is because it is possible to perceive many things without consciously knowing that you've done so.[13] Given what we know about subliminal perception, this isn't so surprising. A good example is seen in tests involving 'subliminal priming'. In one set of experiments, volunteers were asked to respond to words (for example, 'joy', 'death') by pressing a button to say whether the words were pleasant or unpleasant. But there was a catch. The experiments were set up so that the computer showed the volunteer a 'priming' word a moment before they were shown the one that they had to make a decision about. The primer came and went so quickly that no one could see it.[14] Yet the results showed that they *could* see it; they just didn't consciously know it. And it affected their overall perception in a surprisingly powerful way. When the priming word was negative (for example, 'sad'), it slowed down their reactions to positive words (such as 'happy') and sped up their reactions to negative ones (such as 'death'). And the converse was also true: a positive priming word ('joy') sped up the reaction to positive words ('happy') and slowed down the reaction to negative words ('death').[15] So expectation was everything – even (or especially) when they didn't realise they had any expectations at all. The volunteers' subconscious minds were picking up on the fact that something was positive or negative and reacting to it; and this reaction then went on to affect their whole attitude to the following moments – and probably beyond.

But we don't stop with a prediction about how to react, and then wait passively for events to unfold. The body also prepares itself for action and orchestrates the necessary resources to carry them out. Neuroscientist Lisa Feldman Barrett describes this as your body 'budgeting' for what it needs – drawing down resources from its 'bank account' and keeping an 'inventory' of important inputs and outputs. You can feel such body budgeting as it happens through *interoception* – the body's sense of its internal environment that reflects the effects of changing blood flows, muscles preparing for action, the release of hormones and fluxing energy and resource levels.[16] And this moment-by-moment body budgeting often begins with your gut (yes, it really can know best). You might have a feeling of tension as muscles contract, arms or legs get ready to move or the stomach or shoulders begin to tighten. Sometimes this readying is subtle and barely detectable. Sometimes it is not so subtle, and you might become aware of your limbs changing position, your body's temperature rising or falling, its state of alertness shifting, or perhaps a feeling of butterflies in your stomach, or of tightness or even nausea. It's as if an army is mobilising, getting ready for action. Your whole state of being changes by the second.

Think of what this means for brooding or worry. Brooding consists of churning over past actions, those you might have taken, or think you should have taken. Worry is future action that you think you'll need to take to prevent your fears from coming true. In the middle of the night, when you are tossing and turning, you are living out – genuinely experiencing – a series of simulations (or photo bursts) that are rehashes of past actions or ones you have yet to take. Your body is preparing itself, readying its resources and marshalling its forces, ready for actions that you are unlikely to carry out – and certainly not at that moment. No wonder you're tossing and turning. The same is true for other unpleasant states of mind. Anxiety and stress are also manifestations of a body preparing for action – endlessly, fruitlessly. Depression and exhaustion reflect a body that has blown through its budget and more besides.

Feeling tones play a fundamental role here. They both affect and are affected by these processes. It's circular. All too often, viciously circular. The intensity and direction of the feeling tone give direction and urgency to your imagined action. And these imagined actions, in turn, make your mental models feel even more compelling. They feel solid. Real. Like there's no escape. And your body seems to confirm it: look – it's getting ready . . . In fact, much of what exhausts you *is* your body preparing for actions that you simply do not need to take, and probably never will. As if it's endlessly calling up troops for battle, then asking them to stand down.

But it doesn't have to be this way. The aim of Week Five is to bring you closer to the source of your difficulties, closer still to their resolution. You'll do this, firstly, by tuning in to the natural ebb and flow of your feeling tones, then watching as your mind and body gear up for action. Secondly, you will explore what happens when you let go of the need to take action by gently saying to yourself, 'No action needed right now.' Within the context of mindfulness, those five words are some of the most powerful in the English language.

Practices for Week Five

- **Feeling-tone Moment by Moment Meditation** – practise on at least six days out of the next seven for either ten minutes twice per day (meditation 5.1) or twenty minutes once a day (meditation 5.2). Once you're familiar with the instructions, feel free to use the minimal instructions (Mi) version (5.4) or simply use the sound of bells. On at least one day this week, practise for thirty minutes (meditation 5.3).

- **Everyday Mindfulness Practice: Noticing the Feeling Tone in Everyday Life** – practise on at least six days out of the next seven. You might like to begin with three or four activities before steadily increasing their number. Use the audio guidance (meditation 5.5) for the first few days to familiarise yourself with the practice.

All meditations for this week can be found at littlebrown.co.uk/deeper-mindfulness/week-5

The meditations can also be found on the authors' website at franticworld.com/deeper-mindfulness

As you carry out the Feeling-tone Moment by Moment meditation, try to remember that although feeling tones are a constant part of your experience, they can appear and disappear extremely rapidly, so the aim is not to capture every single one, but only those that strike you immediately. In the meditation this week, you'll therefore be invited to use the breath as a pacemaker; as a gentle and regular reminder to tune in to the feeling tone. But not to tune in to the feeling tone of the breath *per se*; nor *only* tune in to the feeling tone at one specific point in the breath's cycle. The feeling tone might arise anywhere within body – or mind – and appear at any moment and be gone the next. Your task is simply to see if you can be aware of it, whenever or wherever it appears; but especially to focus on the feeling tone at the (usually quiet) moment at the end of the out-breath.

You might like to keep a record of what you learn each day. If you keep a journal or diary, you might find it helpful to make a note about how things went: any difficulties, delights or discoveries that you experienced.

The Noticing the Feeling Tone in Everyday Life exercise asks you to become aware of the feeling tones of the various activities that you carry out as you move through your day (see box page 180). You might initially choose only a handful of activities, such as walking into the kitchen to make a drink, eating a meal or brushing your teeth. As you go through the week, you might like to increase the number of things you pay attention to in this way. See if you can also notice any reactions to what's happening. These might manifest as a wish to hold on to or dampen a pleasant moment, get rid of an unpleasant one, tune out of a neutral moment or a sense of restlessness appearing because you feel bored. In the last case, you might react by looking for stimulation – for example, by turning on the TV or radio or perhaps looking for something to eat or drink. Sometimes you'll only become aware of a moment's feeling tone by its 'footprints in the sand' – that is, the effect it has after it's gone; so you might find that you only notice a neutral feeling tone after you have turned on the radio or checked your phone. If this happens, even repeatedly, try not to criticise yourself. It is perfectly normal, even if you find that you've become 'lost in your head'. When it does happen, as best you can, gently note the tonality of the moment in which you 'woke up' from your stream of thoughts and actions. Then, take a pause, register and allow the feeling tone, and consciously choose what to do next rather than simply being driven by habit. You should also aim to do this practice during the 'spaces in between' your day-to-day activities, such as when you are walking somewhere or standing waiting for someone (or something).

Feeling-tone Moment by Moment Meditation

In this meditation, we'll be cultivating awareness of 'feeling tone' by learning to attend closely to the subtle sense of pleasantness or unpleasantness that comes with each moment.

Preparation

1. Sitting so that your posture embodies a sense of wakefulness, bring your attention to whatever is to be your anchor for this sitting: the contact with the floor, the contact with whatever you're sitting on, the contact of hands on your lap or thighs, your breathing.

2. Then after a while, when you're ready, deliberately expand the focus of your awareness to the whole body.

Feeling tone moment by moment

3. As you sit here, see if it's possible to tune in to the feeling tone of each moment – whether it's pleasant, unpleasant or neutral, registering it breath by breath. Just towards the end of the out-breath, as the breath is almost finished and there's a short pause before you take the next in-breath, make a gentle note of how this moment is for you: does it feel pleasant, unpleasant or neutral?

4. Continue to register a subtle sense in body and mind of whether each moment is pleasant, unpleasant or neutral at the end of each out-breath. When you sense the feeling tone, if it's pleasant, say to yourself, 'It's OK to like this.' If it's unpleasant, say, 'It's OK not to like this.'

5. And when you find that your mind gets busy planning or worrying about the future, or gets busy going over the past, say to yourself inwardly, 'No action needed right now'; or 'No action needed at this moment' (or whatever phrase seems right for you).

6. If it feels too difficult to notice feeling tone on every breath, let go of this for a while, and allow the attention to return to your anchor (feet, seat, hands, breath), returning to register feeling tone on the out-breath when you feel ready to do so.

Ending

7. And for the last few moments of the sitting, come back to focus on your breathing or chosen anchor, remembering

that cultivating the ability to register each moment as pleasant or unpleasant gradually brings a deeper sense of how things are for you right now, and a deeper willingness to allow them to be just as they are, without getting caught up in imagined action and reaction. And in the very next moment of your day, you may even find new ways to respond with greater kindness and wisdom to whatever is coming up.

Megan found this week's practices 'liberating', helping her to let herself off the hook of self-criticism. It was, she said, 'a bit of a revelation'.

'I could almost "see" how I'd been torturing myself with perfectionism and a desire to please others. It soon became pretty clear that my *unpleasant* feelings of frustration and irritation would kick-start the horrible thoughts that I had about myself – thoughts about how useless I am, how I always find simple things difficult and how I always let others down. Except that this time I managed to sense and actually feel the feeling tones appearing and then I was able to watch as they just ... went quiet. For the first time in *forever*, I was able to stop beating myself up and torturing myself over my "failings".

'The secret for me was using the out-breath as a cue to pay attention to my feeling tones,' said Megan. 'Such regularity is essential for me because I'm so easily distracted. And then I get frustrated and angry when I realise that I've got distracted again. So I used the breath like a quiet metronome – a little reminder to pay attention. It seems so simple now. And it is – if you remember to actually do it. But it really worked for me. I would sit and follow my breathing, breath by breath, and then I would tap into the tonality. I would just watch and name them as pleasant, unpleasant or neutral.

'Some time in the middle of the week, I realised that my body would tighten up quite obviously at the same moment that I noticed a feeling tone. I looked a little closer and discovered that each feeling tone had a kind of "signature". Unpleasantness appeared as tightness in my stomach, right behind my belly button, then it would spread around to my sides. It felt like a little punch and my whole stomach became as tight as a drum. Really, it was that powerful, so I don't know how I managed to miss it before. Neutral ones were a bit *meh*. Hardly noticeable. I only became aware of them later when my mind had chased off after some random thought or other. When I came across a pleasant feeling tone, I'd feel a bit "light" – almost as if I was levitating towards it, however daft that sounds. Kind of like butterflies fluttering about inside me. I'd then start to notice a stream of emotions inside me, from excitement and a sense of longing through to a bitterness that life is not all it should be. Then a little irritation and anger ... "Why do people have to be so selfish?" But then I had another thought. My expectations were too high. My anger arose out of dashed hopes. Somewhere in my past I had started to believe that everyone should behave sensibly and "rationally". I'd really cling to that idea. But, of course, people often don't behave like that. Hardly ever!'

As Megan described, feeling tones can have a physical signature. This is not true of everyone, so don't worry if there are no such sensations, but for some, there might be a slight sense of contraction in the chest, neck, shoulders or throat when unpleasant feeling tones arise, or opening when pleasant tones are around. Or you might find your hands tensing or relaxing.

You might also find little waves of sensations flickering back and forth through the body. Feeling tones can manifest as more or less anything, especially if you have spent many years being unaware of them. Prepare for the unexpected – and to be surprised.

Megan said: 'Each time I breathed out, I would scan my body for sensations. If I felt any, then I could tap into them, pleasant, unpleasant, neutral … gently recognise them, name them and whisper in my mind, "No action needed just now." And I'd just relax. It would *just be*. And then I'd wait for the next out-breath.'

Megan found that simply saying those words to herself – 'No action needed just now' – had a profoundly positive effect that lingered long after the end of the formal meditation. 'Seeing all of this and giving myself the freedom to not get busy, to remind myself that I didn't have to do anything at all, made the feelings evaporate. Good, bad, neutral … I could just let them lie there undisturbed. And they'd just trickle away. It also helped me to see all the different parts of the "bundle" that were triggered by the feeling tones … the raw emotion, along with the thoughts, feelings and sensations. Something odd then happened: it felt as if the initial observation didn't actually exist. It felt as if I'd somehow turned the whole bundle into something it wasn't and then I'd corrected that "mistake".

'The worst thing was that I'd also been turning the pleasant ones into sadness because I always longed for them to stay. Really longed for a little happiness in my life. So I clung to those moments, and, very quickly I'd get worried that they'd go and never come back. But none of that needed to happen. Giving myself the freedom not to act – to not react – made sure that all of the other unpleasant stuff didn't follow on from those moments of pleasantness. Well, for a while, because my mind didn't reach Nirvana. But I felt, deep down, that I was becoming a little happier and more balanced.'

Gradually, Megan became more forgiving towards her own mind. She began to know, first hand, that the feeling tones, and the way that they arise and pass away, are entirely natural. This reminded her that she did not have to react to every passing one. She could simply watch and wait, knowing that another feeling tone would be along in a moment. Simply saying 'No action needed right now' gently broke the link between the feeling tones and her compulsive tendency to get busy. She could take her time to respond. And quite often, she found that the wisest course of action for her *was* to do nothing at all.

Savouring life's pleasant moments

Sharing life's most beautiful moments is so natural that we often do it without thinking.

Phil told us this story: 'Today I saw a beautiful reflection of a tree in a lake near where I was out for a walk with my partner. I did a double take because I might have easily missed it. In the reflection, the blue sky was shimmering through the breezy leaves. I commented on it to my partner. She didn't hear. I called her to look and see. But even then, she didn't seem to see it as I did. I was a bit disappointed, if I'm honest.'

Telling someone else to pay attention like this, to notice a beautiful view, take a photo or telling them to listen to the sound of the waves crashing on a shore, is often a well-intentioned attempt to share and deepen an experience.

This isn't a problem in itself but if it happens again and again, you may find that it erects a subtle barrier between you and the experience you are trying to share. It prevents you from savouring the moment solely for itself.

Experiencing such moments, without the busyness of action, or the need for someone else's appreciation, can be deeply nourishing. At first, this may seem selfish, but it's not. When you are nourished by the small and precious moments of life, those around you also benefit, as you will become more attentive and 'present' for them.

Not everybody experiences streams of pleasant and unpleasant feeling tones. For some, it's quite common to have many neutral ones instead. This happened to Toyah. She felt 'cloaked in indifference'. 'Kind of numb,' she said. 'Not in a bad way – just a kind of light depression but without the negative soundtrack. It seemed to arise out of parenting. I was just too exhausted to find anything pleasant or unpleasant. So I often found myself wondering what the point of the practice was. Nothing seemed to happen. It was all so neutral. So grey.'

Toyah persevered and looked beneath her blanket of indifference. Even boredom could become interesting, she told herself. She remembered teaching this to her son when he was little. If he said, 'I'm bored,' she would say, 'Let's be really bored together and see what happens.'

'After a little while, he'd start making things out of random materials – it was something interesting and creative. I decided to try the same thing with this practice – to pay attention to the boredom of the neutral feeling tones. I realised that I'd been trying too hard. So I acknowledged the situation by saying to myself, "No action needed right now" as a way of waiting to see what happened in my mind and body. After a while, it occurred to me that in a funny kind of way, the neutral feeling tones were similar to being chilled out and on an even keel. They meant I was just not excited. Not unhappy or depressed – just not excited. So things were just "softer" than I expected. And I discovered that this has an attraction all of its own; that I didn't have to be "amped up" or "on the go" all of the time; that there is a state that is neither excited nor depressed but somewhere soft in between. And sometimes this can be a comforting place to be.'

I can only be happy when ...

Relentlessly striving for certain predefined goals is one of life's major sources of unhappiness and distress, and a great many people don't realise the extent to which they make their happiness dependent on a specific outcome.

Take anything you're looking forward to in the next twelve months (going on holiday, buying a new house or car, finishing an important project). How much do you believe that you can only be happy if you achieve this goal or, to put it another way: do you think you could still be happy even if you do not achieve it? Those who are highly dependent on most, or all, of their plans turning out well tend to be more narrowly focused on how things *must* be. They act with less awareness and are more reactive and judgmental. In short, less mindful. Those who say they could be happy even if things did not turn out exactly as they were hoping, tend to act with greater awareness and are less reactive and judgmental. They are more mindful.[17]

This association affects everyday living, too. Do you recognise the tendency to make your happiness depend on a certain thing happening? The shop having your favourite sandwich; being in time for your appointment; your colleague smiling at you; getting past this slow truck on the highway …

If you feel your happiness depends on such things, then you end up putting too much weight on achieving them, even the relatively small and insignificant things. In so doing, you squander your body budget on irrelevancies, ensuring that there's little energy left for paying attention to the world and enjoying each moment. So you end up not tasting your food, seeing the clouds in the sky or hearing the rustle of leaves on a beautiful autumn day. The list of missed everyday delights is endless. Nor do you notice your tiredness growing and the irritability and short-temperedness that can gradually undermine even the strongest of relationships.

Some can find it hard to use the out-breath as a cue to tune in to the feeling tone. You might find yourself looking too hard, 'hunting' for the pleasant or the unpleasant. You might find yourself striving hard to 'get it right'. It's then quite natural to think that you won't be able to do this for the whole week. If this happens, try to remember that you can return to your chosen anchor – the one that you used in Week One (see page 67) – at any time should you need to steady yourself. You need not rely on the out-breath – or even the breath at all.

Leila also had difficulties noticing feeling tones. This surprised her as she hadn't experienced this in previous weeks. She became increasingly frustrated with herself and the circular, repetitive thoughts that appeared in her mind: 'I can't do this a moment longer, certainly not all week ... I'll go mad.' She steadied herself and smiled at the situation – how the thought, 'I'll go mad' really shouted for her attention and how 'catastrophising' it was. She became aware of the tension in her jaw and shoulders created by the thoughts and decided to take a different tack. She began by spending a few minutes using her feet as an anchor (which she had chosen in Week One) before returning to her out-breath. This worked especially well if her mind became distracted. In this case, she would register the feeling tone of the moment, then for the next five breaths she would see whether and how it changed. Then she became intrigued by the slight pause between the moment when the out-breath was complete and the beginning of the in-breath. She was able to appreciate this moment of relative 'silence' when there were very subtle pleasant or unpleasant echoes of thoughts or feelings. Such moments allowed her to hold them in a larger and quieter space.

In such stillness, the sense of the 'me' who wants things to be a certain way can relax and move aside. You begin to notice the thoughts and sensations that you don't like, which normally lie hidden, but which you try to push away none the less without realising it. When this happens, you might like to check in with your body. Can you feel the body budget readying for action? Such aversion may feel like a pressure in your body, pushing something away, or perhaps slight feelings of tension, flinches or generalised defensiveness. Alternatively, you might notice a thought or an idea that has a 'pull' to it – like, 'I want people to like me', 'I want to succeed' or 'I want to meet someone who will love me.' In such times, if you pay attention to your body, see if you can feel a sense of it 'rallying the troops' to go out and get something you want or need. Does it feel like a tightness in your stomach? Or perhaps a grasping fist in your gut? Or maybe tension in your shoulders or a tightening of your throat? Your hearing might become a little more acute and your skin more sensitive. You may find that your body lets you know more clearly than your conscious mind the thoughts that cause you anxiety or desire – and many other things besides.

Noticing the Feeling Tone in Everyday Life

This week, as you move through your normal daily activities, notice any moments when you become aware of the feeling tone of what's happening.

1. You may find it helpful during the 'spaces in between', for example, when you're walking somewhere or when you are sitting or standing as you wait for somebody or something. As you do this, pay attention to the feel of your feet as they make contact with the ground. Feel the air on your face, arms and legs as you walk or stand.

2. Whatever you find, make space for your feeling tones, whether they feel pleasant or unpleasant. Notice any bundles of feelings, sensations, thoughts and action plans. How do they change from moment to moment? Be kind to yourself as you ground yourself in the present moment and continue the activities of your day.

3. Do you notice any *reaction* to what's happening? A wish
    to hold on to or deepen a pleasant moment or to dampen
    it? If something is unpleasant, do you find yourself brood-
    ing on it or trying to get rid of it? If a moment is more
    neutral, do you find yourself tuning out because it feels
    like there is 'nothing going on'?

4. These feeling tones are perfectly natural, so note them
    with kindness; saying inwardly on the out-breath, 'It's OK
    not to like this' or, 'It's OK to like this.'
    Explore what happens if you add 'No action needed
    right now' on an out-breath before continuing with the
    next moment of your day.

5. With practice, you may see this process more clearly
    and enjoy expanding the space between the momentary
    feeling tone and your reaction to it. You may notice that
    the reactivity pulse loosens its grip when you simply say,
    'It's OK to like this' or, 'It's OK not to like this', followed
    by, 'No action needed right now.'

Bringing the feeling-tone practice into everyday life can be profoundly important. After all, these are the moments when you
will really need to be aware of them.

Mo tells of the first time he used the practice 'in the wild',
rather than in the tranquillity of his meditation. He was due to
give an important address at work. It was an all-day meeting,
and he was scheduled to talk just before lunch, but the previous
speakers were running later and later, the room was too warm
and he realised that he was going to either end up shortening his

talk or going into the dreaded after-lunch slot, when everyone is half-asleep.

As the morning unfolded, he noticed he was tuning in quite naturally to his feeling tones. 'I was anxious,' he said. 'So I assumed they would all be unpleasant, but there were some pleasant moments, too. I enjoyed being with my colleagues and these meetings are often valuable. So I felt both valued and curious about what I would learn during the meeting.'

When an unpleasant moment arrived, he found himself saying, 'It's OK for it to be like this' and then, 'No action needed at this moment.' And by and large, he found himself becoming less anxious and more attentive to the other speakers. This played to his advantage, as they decided to fit his talk in before lunch, even though they were running late.

'You could almost see everyone slump with disappointment when they realised that they were going to be late for lunch – and would probably have to return early, too. I seized the initiative by asking everyone to stand up and stretch for a minute or so before I started. That livened everyone up and gave me space to think. I realised that I could cut out a lot of what I was going to say because others had already covered it, and this meant that I was able to really focus on the main points. I became quite nervous at several points during the talk because I was "ad-libbing" and worried a lot about losing my place in the talk. I dealt with this by pausing for a moment and this added a dramatic impact to the points I was making. Thankfully, the audience didn't have a clue what I was really doing, which was using those moments to drop my attention to my feet (the feet don't get nervous, my meditation teacher says) and focusing on how they felt as they made contact with the floor. This made me feel strong, solid and grounded. I then briefly tuned in to the feeling tones in my body and said in my mind, *It's OK. No action needed right now.*'

In this instance, the practice worked to everyone's advantage. They all ended up going to lunch on time, and congratulated Mo on his graciousness in cutting short his talk. What's more, everyone paid attention to it because it was so brief and focused. Reflecting afterwards, Mo said the practice helped him to stay present and to see through the noise of his compulsions to react. 'It helped me to take wise action,' he said.

CHAPTER TEN

Week Six: Bad Weather Flying

The young man stuffed six bars of chocolate into his fleecy leather jacket. He climbed into the cockpit of the Pitcairn biplane, pulled down his goggles and gave the signal to start the engine. A few minutes later, he was bouncing along the grassy runway in New Jersey before his little plane began climbing, ever so slowly, towards the sunlit clouds and on towards California.

The year was 1930 and the pilot was sixteen-year-old Robert Buck. It was the first of fourteen flying records for the young man. In his early twenties, Bob Buck began flying bigger planes – DC-2s and DC-3s – battling ice, fog, turbulence and thunderstorms, and acquiring the skills that would make him the leading expert in navigating such weather. Just the chapter titles of his 1970 pilots' 'bible', *Weather Flying*,[1] create a sense of exploration and adventure: 'Checking Weather and the Big

Picture', 'Turbulence and Flying It' and 'You are the Captain'. Some headings give gentle warnings – 'It's farther than you think' and 'Weather uses fuel'. Others sound reassuring: 'Weather is mostly good', 'How do you feel?' and 'Keep calm'. Now, with the book in its fifth edition, his son (also a pilot) takes up the story:

'If you flew enough with the guy who wrote *Weather Flying*, you soon learned this weather and flying relationship was a big deal. His enthusiasm for the fascinating riddle of weather was infectious, and one quickly learned that heeding it not only made flying work better, it also kept pilot and airplane safe to fly another day.'[2]

Robert loved difficult weather, and didn't see it as an adversary to be conquered. He would always fly with it, never against it, harnessing its power to his advantage. He'd use rising air currents to gain height and save fuel; tack through weather systems to speed his journey; and deal with turbulence and storms by accepting their presence and working with them, or around them, rather than confronting them directly. Every difficulty, every storm, just like every period of calm, was seen as an opportunity to learn, to hone essential skills.

Decades later, Robert's daughter, Ferris, began putting these principles into practice in her meditation classes. During one of our early visits to the University of Massachusetts Medical Center, one of us (Mark) sat in on a class taught by Ferris.[3] The class was more than halfway through an eight-week course of Mindfulness-based Stress Reduction (MBSR) and some of the participants were very open about their overwhelming moods, their negative thoughts and the challenges in their lives. Those of us who were steeped in the therapy tradition knew what to do as we heard their stories; we would work alongside them to find a way of gradually challenging negative thinking with behavioural assignments. But Ferris didn't make that move at all. She took a radically different approach – one that encouraged participants to *allow* difficult thoughts and feelings to simply be there, to bring a kindly awareness to them and to adopt a more 'welcoming' stance, rather than one focused around a 'need to solve'. We also saw that the approach of Ferris and her colleagues was nothing like the popular stereotype of meditation – that it is a way to clear the mind, or to escape from or shut out unwanted thoughts or feelings. Instead, she encouraged participants to know and to learn from their own direct experience; that fighting against unwanted thoughts, feelings and painful bodily sensations often creates more tension and inner turmoil.

We learned from Ferris's classes – and from those of her colleagues – that mindfulness taught people how to cultivate a wholly different relationship to their thoughts, feelings, impulses and bodily sensations. It taught that thoughts were simply mental events – not 'you' or some kind of concrete reality. This realisation reconnects you to your own inherent wisdom and kindness. It helps you to see that your turbulent moods are entirely understandable; a weather pattern to be navigated. Ferris's approach became a central feature of the treatment we were developing, which later became known as Mindfulness-based Cognitive Therapy. As demand for MBCT increased exponentially around the world, when research trials showed it to be one of the most powerful treatments ever developed for preventing depression, we needed to train new teachers, so Ferris began teaching alongside Zindel Segal and Mark Williams, influencing for ever the way that MBCT developed. Although Ferris died in 2019, this book is a lasting testament to her, our teacher, colleague and friend. As you do the practices in this programme, you are feeling her influence on this Feeling Tone course, too. Through this, you are only a few steps away from her father's *Weather Flying*.

Which brings us to the theme of this week. It's time to learn how to do your own weather flying; to begin dealing skilfully with turbulent emotions. Although at first this might seem a little daunting, you already have all the skills you will need. In Week One, you practised steadying your mind and using different anchors for your attention. In Week Two, you practised sustaining your attention by deliberately taking a pause when your mind was distracted. In Week Three, you learned to observe the feeling tone of whatever arose in your mind and body. In Week Four, you practised allowing the feeling tone to be just as you found it, deliberately dissolving the tendency to overreact, by gently saying to yourself, 'It's OK to like this' or, 'It's OK not like this.' Last week, you took this process a little further by focusing on the natural changeability of your feeling tones, and then learned how to dissolve their unreasonable demands by gently saying inwardly, 'No action needed right now.' This week, you will bring all these skills together. You will learn to welcome those times when emotions threaten to overwhelm you; to see them as opportunities to practise your own weather flying.

Before embarking on this week's practices, it's helpful to know how to deal with something that can undermine all your efforts, adding to your turbulence, and making an emotional storm last even longer. You'll know it as unkindness. If you listen to your mind when you are in distress, there is often an undercurrent of self-criticism. Unpleasant thoughts might appear – such as 'I shouldn't be feeling like this'; 'I should be stronger than this'; 'I thought I was over it'; 'Pull yourself together.' These thoughts, and others like them, are an attempt to snap yourself out of your mood, but few of us notice just how unkind they really are. Imagine saying those things to a good friend who is distressed, vulnerable, depressed or grieving. You wouldn't consider that for a single moment. You would know how painful these words could be, and also that they would be totally counterproductive. Such cruelty would make your friend feel worse, erode their self-confidence and further weaken them. So why persist in saying these things to yourself? It is probably because you think it will help. Nobody attacks themselves in this way thinking that it will inflict harm. Quite the opposite. You want to get rid of your unpleasant feelings and assume that being unkind is a form of 'tough love' that 'just works' because such storms can sometimes ease off a little in the short term. But they don't truly ease off; you have simply stunned yourself into submission – much like a boxer who jabs their opponent on the chin. And you might come to think that you have battled such feelings successfully, whereas, in reality, you have simply distracted and weakened yourself, setting the stage for the next cycle of negative thinking.

But there is an alternative. You can enhance your inner strength by cultivating kindness towards your distressed mind and heart. And that is what you will be doing this week. You will begin by practising the Kindness meditation and then you will draw on your enhanced resources as you start working with your difficult emotions using the Exploring Difficulty meditation and the Everyday Mindfulness practice.

Practices for Week Six

- **Kindness Meditation** – should be carried out on Days One, Three and Five of this week (meditation 6.1). Once you are familiar with the instructions, use the minimal instructions (Mi) version (meditation 6.2).
- **Exploring Difficulty Meditation** – should be carried out on Days Two, Four and Six of this week for either ten minutes twice a day (meditation 6.3) or twenty minutes once a day (meditation 6.4). Once you're familiar with the meditation, you can use the minimal instructions (Mi) version (6.5) or simply the sound of bells.
- **Practise the Kindness or Exploring Difficulty Meditation** (6.2 or 6.5), or any other meditation from a previous week, on at least one day this week, for thirty minutes.
- **Everyday Mindfulness Practice: Turning Towards Difficulty** should be carried out on at least six days this week, or whenever you become aware of unpleasant feeling tones (see box page 208 for detailed guidance). You might like to listen to meditation 6.6, to help you with the first few days of this practice.

All meditations for this week can be found at littlebrown.co.uk/deeper-mindfulness/week-6

The meditations can also be found on the authors' website at franticworld.com/deeper-mindfulness

Kindness Meditation

In this meditation, you'll be invited to take time to wish yourself well — to treat yourself with kindness in the midst of whatever is happening in your life.

Preparation

1. Start by grounding yourself for a few minutes, attending to the sensations of the breath at the nose, chest or abdomen.

2. Then, for a few minutes more, come to rest in awareness of the whole body, as you sit here.

Remembering acts of kindness by others

3. When you're ready, see if it's possible to bring to mind someone for whom you feel a sense of love or friendship, from now or from your past. This might be a good friend, a parent or grandparent, a child or grandchild — someone close and with whom your relationship is not too complicated; someone who's easy to love. If a person does not come readily to mind, you may recall a single act of kindness; a time when someone who showed love or care in what they did for you, and made a difference in that moment. Or you might find that a pet comes to mind — a friendly being that warms your heart.

4. See them clearly in your mind's eye and allow them to remain in your heart for these moments …

    … allowing the felt sense of kindness and friendship between you to surround and bathe you in its warmth.

Bringing kindness to yourself

5. When you are ready, see if it is possible to bring the same sense of kindness and friendship to yourself – silently saying to yourself:

   May I be safe and well;
   May I live in peace;
   May I live with ease and kindness.

6. In this way, you are bringing to yourself the same sense of kindness and friendship that a beloved friend or family member would wish for you. If it is difficult, see what it feels like to use your own name instead of 'I'. Using your own name can feel very different. You might also like to explore putting a hand (or both hands) on your heart region as you say these phrases.

Kindness in the midst of things

7. Sometimes it's difficult to wish yourself well, perhaps because of what's going on in your life. See how it is to acknowledge this difficulty, adding words to help this:[4]

   May I be safe and well in the midst of this;
   May I be at peace in the midst of this;
   May I live with ease and kindness in the
       midst of this.

8. Even if it seems difficult to wish yourself well in this way, doing the practice regularly can gradually, over time, open the mind and heart towards a new possibility: that the harsh things you say or think about yourself are not the last word. You may be loved more than you'll ever think or know.

Ending

9. And now, let go of these intentions, and come back to the body as a whole, sitting here; resting in awareness itself. Allow your body to be just as it is, and allow yourself to be just as you are, complete and whole.

One of the kindest things you can do for others is to first be kind to yourself. Many rebel against this idea because there is something buried in the culture of Western civilisation – and increasingly, elsewhere, too – that makes this very difficult. Self-compassion and understanding towards oneself are often seen as weak, self-indulgent, selfish even. Being tough on yourself, relentlessly pushing your limits and showing yourself no quarter are seen as ways of achieving greatness. Leila suffered from this problem for many years.

'"No time for rest on a dying planet", was my motto,' said Leila. 'I work for a loud and brash environmental group. We are in constant conflict with big companies and many governments around the world. I would go into work every day and fight, fight, fight. I knew that what we were doing was morally right, and this always gave me huge amounts of energy and the determination to push myself forwards. And it worked for many years, until, one day, it didn't. One morning, I just felt completely knackered and broken inside. I could barely get out of bed. Stress then forced me to take a month off work during the heat of a major campaign and I hated myself for it. I spent the next year trying to get back into full-on campaigning mode, but I kept running into the buffers. Every time I started moving forwards, I'd run out of puff again. It was awful.'

Leila eventually discovered that a little part of herself was crying inside: 'It was tragic to feel it. Something delicate and beautiful was dying. I was responsible. It felt like I was some kind of abusive partner. I'd been beating the hell out of this little child inside. I'd been "gaslighting" and bullying her. I suppose I was doing it with the best of intentions, to get the best out of myself, so that I could help protect the environment, but it still meant that I was in an abusive relationship with myself.

'I realised that I needed to change before I destroyed myself – or became indistinguishable from the people and organisations that I was trying to beat. I thought it was going to be tough to change, but what was the alternative? I realised early on that it would be a whole lot easier than continuing to live a life riven with anger and stress and one that had replaced genuine intimacy with bored indifference.

'Although it wasn't "easy" to change my approach to life, it was nowhere near as difficult as I'd imagined either. I'd been so hard on myself that showing myself even the smallest amount of kindness and compassion paid back very quickly. Almost from one day to the next I began to relax – to just float on what felt like a sea of kindness. It was odd. All the negativity drained out of my mind, and I felt a kind of healing silence. It was like the negative, critical voice had gone on holiday. I felt a beautiful calmness that allowed me to reconnect with myself on some fundamental level.'

It wasn't all plain sailing, though. As Leila's strength and resilience returned, so did her old ways and approaches. But rather than fight them, she welcomed them instead. She saw them for what they were: an attempt by one part of herself to help and protect the whole of her in the only way they knew how. 'Each time they returned, I thanked them for their efforts and then they seemed to dissolve and leave me alone for a while. I began to see them as begrudgingly taking their place on the back row of my life. And as mad as it sounds, I reassured them that if I needed their help, then I would ask for it.'

Leila encountered some other difficulties, too. She found the words to the Kindness meditation a little odd. Some of them jarred because she wasn't used to bringing love and kindness to herself. If, like Leila, you find the guided practice sounding a little strange (or not the sort of language you would normally use), feel free to adapt the words for yourself, so that they feel more 'you'. Perhaps you could see the practice like the gym exercise (see page 80). By adapting the words, you may then find some phrases staying with you during the day. Leila found she could relate most to the words 'ease and kindness'.

'There was a distinct feeling of warmth and of "letting go" in my heart and chest area, and after doing the practice, I felt calm, uplifted, held. Then, later that day, I realised that when I was more loving to myself, I was more likely to let go of the pent-up anguish that I usually carry around on my shoulders. And guess what? I felt more genuinely friendly and loving towards others, too.'

Leila had discovered something reported by many others. That kindness helps you to let go of the pent-up anxiety and stress that weigh you down – the very same anxiety and stress that make you combative towards others, too. So practising kindness is not only good for you, but benefits everyone around you as well. Increasingly, research is showing the same effect. For example, people who have completed a mindfulness programme are quicker to give up their seat in a waiting room to other people on crutches.[5] It turns out that such positive attributes as kindness and friendliness are '360-degree' qualities.[6] So if we embody these and bring them to the person we often find the hardest to love – ourselves – we will frequently find ourselves spontaneously being altruistic towards others. It can become an ongoing dance of friendship, kindness and generosity.

But not everyone gets such quick relief from their troubles with the Kindness meditation. For some, the mind's weather patterns are too turbulent and take time to settle down. 'At first,' said Lou, 'I thought this Kindness meditation wasn't helpful. I think there was too much going on in my life, too many distractions for me to notice any benefits. I've also been so badly hurt in the past that it felt like nothing would really change, no matter what I did. But after a few days, something shifted. I got a glimpse ... a sense that I have choices. And it's strange, but the only way of saying it is that I gave that little child in me permission to feel miserable and scared. I reassured her that it's OK not to like it. This seemed to give me more space – more options. After this, I went back to tracking the feeling tone on each out-breath. I began to really value that moment of stillness at the end of the out-breath and before the next in-breath. I realised: no action needed in this moment. Phew! Now, after all these weeks of practice, the out-breath is a starting point to a new opportunity in every moment. I realised that I don't usually practise kindness towards myself at all. Just the opposite. I have always been highly critical, and I reserve the main criticism for myself.'

Relentless criticism is another 360-degree attitude. Critical towards yourself; critical towards others. And without knowing it, such criticism leads to a feeling of 'contraction' that, in turn, reduces creativity and so to feelings of being 'stuck'. These then trigger more habitual reactions that close down your options further, leading to deeper feelings of contraction and an even greater sense of frustration. It's a vicious cycle that propels you ever further downwards.

'I knew all this,' said Lou, 'but somehow, I couldn't embody it. I kept on rebelling against the idea that it was wrong to criticise. How on earth did people think the modern world got built if it wasn't for criticism? Criticism of flawed ideas, approaches, designs and stuff in general . . . If people don't criticise how can things get improved?'

While understandable, Lou's concerns were simply misunderstandings about mindfulness and how change comes about. Firstly, it isn't 'wrong' to criticise. It is simply unhelpful and counterproductive to engage with relentless criticism – especially self-criticism. Instead, it is often better to stand back and observe from a wider perspective. In this way, criticism is transformed into wise discernment, and takes up its rightful place in your life – as a marker for change, rather than a stick with which to beat yourself. If you stand back and observe, you are far more likely to see solutions, rather than problems. Sometimes, if you overly focus on a problem, it can end up filling your entire field of vision, so the actual solution is obscured.

Like Leila, Karl decided to tweak the Kindness meditation to make it more relevant to himself. He found focusing on the kindness of others too difficult. The complexity of their overall character, and his relationship to them, was a little overwhelming and he found it more helpful to bring to mind a specific act of kindness rather than a person. He therefore decided to focus on a moment from when he was eight years old. He brought to mind a teacher at his new school who noticed that he was lost and alone in the playground and guided him back to his own class. It may only have been a small act of kindness but it made a huge difference in that moment of distress and he's never forgotten it.

Sometimes even smaller changes to the meditation can yield surprising results. Avril discovered this, but in a different way. She found it hard to wish herself well at first. It was almost as if she didn't want to be the centre of her own thoughts. But then her meditation teacher suggested that she use her own name. Although she found it strange to say, 'May Avril be safe and well in the midst of this' she did find that it made it easier to do the meditation. She said it separated the Avril from the 'me', so that it became easier to wish that person well. And the words 'in the midst of this . . .' made it easier for her to realise that although there may be bad times, it was still possible to find kindness in even the most difficult of moments.

KINDNESS, HAPPINESS

As you proceed through this week, you may come to realise that happiness often arises all by itself. You don't have to do a thing. You may have spent months – or years – striving to be happy, endlessly pursuing it, often to no avail. Such pursuit tends to create a certain shallowness of experience. A flavour of happiness that quickly evaporates. You could call it pleasure rather than true happiness. This triggers a fear that it will soon melt away, a longing for it to remain, leaving you with a craving for a deeper, more authentic and longer-lasting happiness. Kindness cultivates something different. You could call it joy. Such joy often arises out of the small things: out of kindness to yourself and to others; out of a life well lived.

Avril came to understand this – that her endless pursuit of happiness had chased it away: 'Instead of trying to be happy ... I just decided to be kind to myself and to others. This made a huge difference. It helped me calm down. It was quite a profound realisation, like a light bulb going on. I was riding on the bus into town and realised that I was exhausting myself trying to be happy all the time. You know, I spent a fortune on clothes, make-up, nights out, fancy holidays, being seen with "the right people" in "the right places". I would always strive to ape those social media "influencers", but it didn't really do much for me. Not deep down. It was actually quite a struggle to keep up! Oh, don't get me wrong, I loved it for a while – a short while ... but it was all a distraction, really. Since then, I've come to see that it's so much easier to bring a little kindness to myself and to others. I realised that I was feeling driven to find the elusive magic bullet that would make me happy. And then I suddenly saw that I didn't have to do all of that. I didn't need to strive. I could just be myself for a while and see what happened.'

Avril's insight is significant. Happiness can be a goal that feels urgent and can consume vast amounts of energy trying to make it happen. Busy, busy, busy. You can easily end up creating more suffering for yourself as you relentlessly pursue happiness. Your mind is trying to help you by gearing up and planning actions, generating 'what-ifs' to bring you closer to bliss. But whatever it tries to do simply does not help. When you realise how much suffering you are creating for yourself – when you start to see it almost as an addiction – this is the perfect moment to let go of the habit. You will suddenly see that there's another way: you can instead try being kind to yourself. Right now. You don't have to buy yourself luxuries or even little treats, nor strive to be a certain way; you can simply bring kind-hearted warmth and awareness to yourself at appropriate points in the meditations and throughout your day. You can let go of punishing yourself. And you can begin by relaxing into your own skin; by accepting yourself with all your faults and failings.

As you get to know your mind's weather patterns, you may find you are more vulnerable at certain points than others during the day. Felicity realised that she was most vulnerable in the moments after she first woke up. She decided to experiment. Normally, she would try to spur herself on with self-critical thoughts, such as 'Come on, get a move on', 'Don't be lazy' and 'What will everyone think?' This week she decided to try bringing kindness and understanding to herself instead. In previous weeks, she had deliberately paid attention to her mind's weather patterns before rushing into her day. Through this, she had learned something extremely valuable. She had believed, and would always tell herself, that she had a panic attack every morning. When she paid closer attention, though, she quickly learned that it did not happen every morning, but only about half the time. She soon began to see the 'nuances' of the weather as well: she would quietly note in her mind: 'Here is pleasantness in the body; here is unpleasantness in the thought stream; here is pleasantness in the environment.' She began to notice little things, like the gentle flowing air from a window on a cool summer's morning. Birdsong, too. So her early mornings were not nearly as bad as she'd been telling herself.

Then, one morning, she awoke with pain and stiffness in her

back and shoulders. She assumed that she'd had yet another nightmare. Normally, this would make her heart sink as she realised that she was about to start yet another day feeling tired and listless. Such bad feelings would then spill forwards into a prediction: 'This is going to be a bad day ...' She knew what would happen next. But this time she simply labelled it 'Unpleasant'. Then, 'It's OK not to like this.'

'And it dissolved. Just like that,' Felicity said. 'The practice was gradually helping me to befriend my experience. Maybe even to honour it. And then I went into the day with more self-kindness. I'd normally be so unkind to myself in the morning. I'd bully and cajole myself. Demand that I push myself into action. It turned out that adopting a more gentle, warm and kind attitude towards myself helped to soften these demands. It gave me the time for these moments – both pleasant and unpleasant – to pass of their own accord.'

EXPLORING DIFFICULT EMOTIONS

Once you start treating yourself with a little warmth, kindness and compassion, you have the 'fuel on board' to begin to navigate the bad weather – your more difficult and troubling emotions. This is the core aim of this week's Exploring Difficulty meditation (see page 203). But first, it's important to remind yourself about some of the key elements that we discussed in Week One.

Firstly, whenever you approach a difficulty, try to remember that you have a choice about how you wish to proceed. You should only work with a difficulty if you feel you have the capacity and the energy right now. If you feel too tired, or life feels overwhelming, then wait until you feel more capable of working with it. There is no point in gritting your teeth and forcing yourself to meditate through extreme mental or physical distress.

Secondly, you can choose how closely you wish to approach a difficulty. It will also be helpful to decide in advance how you will return to 'safe ground' should you find yourself distressed. Such safe ground might be the sensations in your hands or feet, or of contact with your seat or the floor, or the feelings the breath makes as it flows in and out. Grounding or anchoring yourself in this way will help you to unhook yourself from any unhelpful thought patterns that are fuelling your distressing emotions. In this way, you will learn to explore the full range of experience from the relative safety of physical sensations at one end of the spectrum through to the emotional storms created by turbulent thoughts, memories, images and impulses at the other extreme. This practice invites you to move to and fro along this spectrum at your own pace.

Spontaneous difficulties

Sometimes, difficult feelings will arise spontaneously, and you can practise with these. They will become your teacher. If no difficulties arise, then the meditation invites you to deliberately bring one to mind, and before you start, you might choose to recall something from the last few days you could use as an example. It will be best if you begin with small difficulties in daily life: maybe a misunderstanding or a disagreement, a situation that made you feel irritated, a regret over something that has happened or a worry about something that might happen. It's best to start with small things, because the practice isn't about resolving the biggest problems all at once. It's about learning to 'fly the weather' – gradually turning towards difficulties in a way that helps you to respond skilfully, rather than becoming lost inside a cascade of reactions. And, as Robert Buck pointed out, the weather isn't always kind to pilots.

When a difficult situation or emotion appears in your mind, you then have a number of options. You can simply acknowledge its presence, almost at a distance, before moving back to your anchor (see box opposite for details). Or you can practise sensing it and holding it in a wider context. Alternatively, you can notice where in the body the emotion has appeared. It might be almost anywhere and manifest as almost anything, although it's most likely to appear as an area of tightness, as fluttering muscles, discomfort or even pain. Move your attention right up to it, and into that part of the body, really feeling it. You could try breathing into it – feeling it being massaged by the breath – not to get rid of it, but to put some space around it. All these options provide alternative approaches to the entirely natural habit of avoiding difficult emotions or of blaming yourself for them. Instead, you are learning how to allow things to be just as they are, for a moment longer than you normally would, and this progressively dissolves your difficulties, ultimately granting you the time and the space to make wiser decisions.

Throughout the week's practice, you will also begin to learn how to accept yourself just as you are. You will begin to see that your feelings are a part of nature; that you have a body and a mind that are doing their best to keep you safe in the only way that they know how.

At first, you may not find this practice easy, so throughout the process, remember that your chosen anchor will always be available to you. If a difficulty starts to become overwhelming, you might like to gently ask yourself: 'What else is here, right now, in this moment?' And if you choose, you could try opening your eyes for a few moments.

Now, it is time to begin weather flying.

Exploring Difficulty Meditation

Preparation

1. Start by making yourself comfortable on a stool, a cushion or a chair, so that your posture embodies a sense of dignity, of being present. And let your eyes close or lower your gaze.

2. Ground yourself by choosing your anchors for this practice, then, when you are ready, deliberately expand the focus of your awareness to the whole body.

If difficult emotions arise

3. While you are sitting, if you notice that your attention keeps being pulled away towards painful emotions, you can explore a different approach from what you've practised when distractions have arisen up till now. Instead of bringing the mind back from a thought or feeling, allow the thought or feeling to remain in the mind for a moment, either acknowledging it before returning to your anchor or holding it in awareness – sensing it and also feeling space around it. Or you can go further, noticing where in the body the emotion is showing itself and moving your attention right up to and into this part of the body, breathing into it, surrounding it with kindness.

Bringing a difficulty to mind

4. If nothing is coming up, and you want to explore this new way of turning towards difficulty, then deliberately bring to mind some small problem in your life now or from the past, that causes unpleasant emotions for you ... something you don't mind staying with for a short while: a person, a place, something that happened. It doesn't have to be very big, but something that you are aware of as somewhat unpleasant; something unresolved, perhaps.

Working with the difficulty

5. And whether the difficulty has come by itself or because you have brought it to mind, once it's here, allow it to remain on the workbench of the mind, shifting your attention into the body and noticing any physical sensations that come along with it. These sensations may be very obvious or not so obvious. But see if you can discern what sensations are arising when a difficult emotion is around.

6. Where are these body sensations? Do they have a shape? Where do you experience them most vividly? Do they change from moment to moment? (If no body sensations seem to come with the difficulty, then choose any sensations that are present in your body and practise with these.)

7. Perhaps imagine you could 'breathe into' this region on the in-breath, and 'breathe out' from it on the out-breath;

not to change the sensations, but to explore them and give them space; to sense them clearly, registering their feeling tone, cradling them in awareness as you watch their intensity change and flux from moment to moment.

8. Notice how you are reacting to whatever comes up for you: holding these reactions (which may bring their own thoughts and sensations) in a spacious and compassionate awareness, too, checking in with the feeling tone of the sensations of reaction (pleasant, unpleasant, neutral).

9. Register the feeling tone, whatever it is, breath by breath, remembering that you don't have to like such feelings in the body. Knowing them to be unpleasant is natural. It may be helpful to repeat phrases such as, 'It's OK not to like this.' Then, whatever sensations you find, see if you can be open to them, just as they are.

10. You may find it helpful, on an out-breath, to say inwardly 'No action needed right now', as you hold the sensations, wherever they are in the body, in a gentle and spacious awareness.

11. And, as you stay with the awareness of these bodily sensations for as long as you choose, continue to breathe with them, allowing them to be just as they are, seeing how they unfold and surrounding the sensations with a sense of kindness and compassion; and surrounding yourself with kindness and compassion, too.

12. If you notice that the sensations fade, then choose whether to come back and stay with your anchor points – the feet, seat, hands or breath – or to go around again, bringing the same or a new difficult situation to mind, and when it has arrived in the mind bringing your attention right up to the edge, or inside the bundle of sensations it is creating in the body.

If things feel overwhelming

13. And at any time, if things feel overwhelming or you find yourself simply brooding on things, ask, 'What's my best support right now?' 'What else is here?' and come back to the breath or the feet, seat or hands, until you feel ready either to move back to the practice or to continue on to the next moments of your day. Knowing you have options. Being kind. No right or wrong.

Ending

14. When you are ready, come back to focus on your anchor: the breath or the feet, the seat or your hands. Congratulate yourself for taking this time to explore the edges of what's difficult for you. You are finding ways of responding intentionally, rather than reacting automatically, taking time to cultivate a sense of openness, kindness and compassion even in the midst of difficulties that arise in your life.

EXPECTING THE UNEXPECTED

For many people, the Exploring Difficulty practice can be a
little odd. It can come as a great surprise to find an emotional
difficulty embedded physically in the body. And few expect it to
be so definite and powerful. Nor do they expect to find such a
variety of different sensations.

This was Ana's experience: 'When I brought a difficult situation to mind, I felt a heaviness in my right arm; it felt like it
was made of concrete. Then I realised that I have a tendency to
try and fix what is unfixable and somehow, on this occasion,
my worries for my daughter's marriage had become "fixed"
in my arm. I know it sounds crazy, but this is what happened.
This made me realise that if somebody else's problems were
causing me such strong physical reactions, then it was time for
me to summon the courage to let go, and trust that they have
the ability to handle them. The next time I did the meditation,
I got a different reaction. I sensed a heaviness around my stomach, but as I held it gently, it became light like paper. It felt like
I was being released from an awful lot of worry. I got similar
reactions when I carried these ideas across to the Everyday
Mindfulness practice. Each time I noticed a worry appear – or
any troubling feeling, really – I focused on the physical sensations, where they were in my body, and how they constantly
changed. I alternated between exploring the physical sensations
and grounding myself and then moving back to the sensations
again. It was really helpful for me to ground myself before I
turned towards the difficulty, and then to ground myself again
a short while after. Grounding also helped me to trust myself to
actually cope with life. Being warmer to myself – to give myself

a break from criticism by kindly saying to myself, "It's OK not to like this" – helped with trust, too. I gradually learned to trust that I could do it.'

Everyday Mindfulness Practice: Turning Towards Difficulty

This practice asks you to pay close attention to those moments when you become aware of unpleasant feeling tones. When this happens, gently move your attention to your body and notice where it is reacting and how it is doing so.

1. Spend a few moments paying attention and notice the things that change and those that stay the same.

2. Notice the feeling tones – they may be more variable than you expect.

3. See if there are any reactions to what's happening; there may be a wish to get rid of the unpleasantness. This, in turn, may usher in other sensations in the body – try to explore these as well and see how their feeling tones change from moment to moment. Sometimes you'll only know the feeling tone of a moment by its later impact.

4. In whatever way a difficulty presents itself, remember to gently say inwardly, 'It's OK not to like this', and, on the next out-breath, 'No action needed at this moment.' In this way, you are bringing kindness to your heart and mind – and so, quietly, little by little, making friends again

with those vulnerable aspects of yourself that most need your love and compassion.

5. As you do this practice, if you are willing and have the capacity, allow your attention to remain as steady and open as possible so that you can see clearly what's happening even as emotional turbulence arrives, stays a while and leaves.

6. Try to remember, with as much kindness as your heart can muster, that such steady attention can take some time to learn, but it will pay dividends in the end, so perhaps begin with some of the easier situations.

Sometimes a difficulty takes the form of a shape in the body. Toby said that for him it was a misshapen, heavy, jagged brown stone. 'I could really feel it – fully formed. It was in my chest area. I became aware of my heart beating fast, my breathing shallow, panicky, too. Then I thought, *Is this becoming too much?* I realised it was, so I stood back and "placed it on the workbench of the mind" and said to myself, "It's OK to feel like this." There was a real mixture of emotions ... fear, sadness, anger and frustration. Then I gave it space. More fear and frustration came. Then, noticing that the sensations in the body were changing moment by moment. There was fluttering in the chest, I was breathing faster and shallower again. I said, "It is OK not to like this" and the difficulty moved. It became a pain in the lower right shin that wanted attention and then the next moment the left shoulder went into a little spasm. It all felt like one big unpleasant feeling tone. I kept watching to see if it changed.

I kept patiently watching to see what else was there, to see if the storm of unpleasantness would pass. It did. I noticed that my feet felt alive, tingly, not unpleasant. I realised that I really did have a choice. I could be swept along by the turbulence of unpleasantness or I could ... pay attention. Then I let go on the out-breath with "no action needed right now" and this brought some relief. Bringing attention to the feet, the ground and the aliveness of my body really helped.'

In these ways, Toby was using the practice to intentionally shift along the spectrum of his difficulties: 'Afterwards, it felt like a relief to have gone up close to it, even just for one moment.'

THE DANGER OF FEEDING RUMINATION

Sim found that exploring his difficulties was a frustrating process with little apparent benefit at first. His anxious fears about 'being used' and 'taken advantage of' would often surface during his meditations and then return around bedtime. He struggled to approach such feelings. And, to make matters worse, his previous weeks of meditation had noticeably enhanced his wellbeing, so he felt disappointed as well as frustrated with Week Six. And although he was willing to force himself to do the Exploring Difficulty practice, he did not have the capacity to do it – the rumination within him was just too strong.

If you should feel like this, it's good to remind yourself that you can come back to the practice on another day. You do not have to jump in at the deep end. Even if you just 'dip your toe in the water' with this one, this may be enough to reveal to you an alternative view of your body and mind – that they are part of the natural world that you can witness with curiosity and kindness. It can take time – but there is no rush. And you might find that you are learning more about yourself than you realise, as well as how you can successfully avoid falling into your usual negative habits of thinking and behaving.

This was Sim's experience. He was despondent about having made no apparent progress and this was compounded halfway through the week when he came back late from a work meeting. He was tired and went to get a drink from the kitchen. Dishes were piled up in the sink and none of his housemates had unloaded the dishwasher. Everyone had disappeared to their rooms. He felt the familiar feelings of being used and taken advantage of. 'No one cares, no one lifts a finger to help, no one supports me,' he grumbled to himself. 'Everything is left to me. I'm completely alone. I might as well get used to it ...'

His mood had begun to take the familiar turn for the worse. But on this occasion, he recognised just in time that this thought stream would inevitably trigger a cascade of negativity unless he decided to act out of conscious choice. So instead of allowing the thoughts to run away with him, he gently acknowledged them. He said to himself, 'It's OK not to like this – feeling tired and grumpy is unpleasant. It's OK not to like it. No action needed right now.'

Often, in such situations, it can be very difficult to know how to respond because when it comes to the actions of others, there are just so many possibilities, variables, agendas, attitudes and approaches to consider. And the better at problem-solving you are, the more possibilities are open to you, which makes any decisions far more nuanced and complex. So in the heat of the moment, when you try to think of the best course of action, you can end up making the situation worse rather than better. And, of course, your subconscious self is planning for these eventualities and preparing to act on them, which makes your distress even worse and certainly burns up a lot of energy from your body budget. It's hardly surprising, then, that you may find yourself rebelling against the instruction 'No action needed'. You may find yourself becoming increasingly tense, almost as if you are being pulled in two different directions at once: to act and not to act. This is a tortured place to be. You can feel genuinely riven by indecision. Or compelled to make the wrong decision.

But there is a way out. You can gently remind yourself of the wording of the phrase: 'No action needed *right now.*' What the phrase is inviting you to do is to see if you need to do anything *right now*. And in most cases, you need do nothing at all – and certainly not *right now* in that precise moment. Remembering this can bring enormous relief and transform the situation. Then it becomes not about whether you must respond or not respond, but about the timing of any response. Should you adopt such an approach, you will quite often notice that your body relaxes as soon as you realise that you can indeed act – but you only need do so when the time is right. And in the long run, you might decide that the best course of action is to do nothing at all.

This is what Sim did. He allowed himself to feel the unpleasantness of being aggrieved. And doing this, without criticising himself, opened up a small space in which the grumpy, let-down feelings of loneliness could be held lightly and compassionately. So instead of experiencing a sense of entitlement to get upset, and then responding by angrily pushing away those feelings or criticising himself (and others), he simply allowed them to exist. He just acknowledged their unpleasant feeling tone and let them be.

'And it transformed everything,' he said.

For the next half-hour, the brooding thoughts started up again and again but each time, he reminded himself that 'It was OK not to like them. No action needed right now.' And the more he did so, the less distressed he felt. Instead of spending that evening rehearsing arguments with his housemates, he left the dishes and went to bed. When he got up in the morning, they had been cleared. It turned out that his housemates had also been very tired as one of them had received some sad news, and they had decided to leave the dishes till the morning.

Sim was slowly learning that meditation is a lot like successful weather flying. Robert Buck emphasised that decisions should always be made on a trip-by-trip basis and re-evaluated during every flight: 'With the idea that one crawls before walking, we can teach ourselves to fly weather. It's a progressive process ... We must remain humble for a long time and know when to quit or when not to go.'

For Robert Buck, a safe landing after a storm was nothing more than one you could walk away from. Mindfulness helps us bring that spirit to the turbulence in our lives. Flying the storms of our feelings demands just such skill, patience and non-judgmental kindness. Little by little, the regular practice of mindfulness will allow you to fly the weather and to make safe landings.

CHAPTER ELEVEN

Week Seven:
Reclaiming Your Life

It was the favourite time of the day for Tabby, the family cat. It was early evening and her owners had placed her dinner in the corner of the kitchen where she usually ate. She walked over and began munching delightedly. But then a large box of cornflakes fell from the top shelf and landed with a loud crash beside her. Terrified, she ran out of the kitchen and hid under the living-room sofa. And there she sat for over an hour, quivering with fear, as the family tried to coax her out. For weeks afterwards, Tabby was terrified of that kitchen corner and there was nothing anyone could do to make her eat or drink in that part of the room. Even getting her into the kitchen was something of a struggle.

Although Tabby's behaviour might seem overly neurotic, she was behaving entirely rationally. For good evolutionary reasons, her favourite eating place had acquired an aura of danger. No animal – including we humans – is inclined to go back to a place associated with such unpleasant emotions as fear. It can hang around for a very long time after the initial threat has receded and may even become stronger as time passes. And it needn't be a huge shock that creates such ingrained fear. Even small ones can become incorporated into the mind's mental model of the world, affecting your whole outlook on life, colouring everything that you think, feel, sense and do, so that what starts out as a short-lived disturbance progressively turns into a major issue, building through time. In humans, this may even lead to real mental-health challenges.

In Tabby's case, the initial shock affected her mind's predictions about where was safe or dangerous, and no creature, be they a cat or a human, is likely to test such predictions. And dismissing or confronting them just makes them worse because such an approach serves only to further erode self-confidence and resilience. If Tabby could understand language, her fears would have been compounded if her owners had said harshly, 'Come on, don't be stupid. It was only a box of cornflakes. What's up with you? You can't go through life jumping at shadows like this ...'

But Tabby's owners were wise enough not to force her into eating in the corner of the kitchen she feared so much. Instead, they 'empathised' with her distress and worked to rebuild her confidence. Over a number of weeks, they positioned her food gradually closer and closer to where she'd had her fright, until everything was back to normal. And such an approach can work for us, too.

Moving ever closer to what scares you is rather like what you practised in Week Six. It can also help with other types of avoidance, such as troubling emotions in general and the memory of events that created them.

But there is another type of avoidance that is very common when you are stressed, depressed or exhausted; the type of generalised withdrawal from the world that can be genuinely crippling, and which makes it ever harder to lead a normal life. Such a retreat from life happens when many of the things that you used to enjoy stop being pleasant, so you give up on them, while at the same time, many of the routine tasks that are needed to lead a normal life are left undone. It feels like someone has turned off your motivation switch. It's almost as if your mind has estimated the energy that would be needed to re-engage with life and decided that the cost of the effort is just too high. Then, paradoxically, the things that used to give you pleasure become ever more difficult to contemplate, even though, without them, life feels increasingly shallow, grey and pointless. So it feels impossible to do the very things that would reinvigorate your life and lift you out of depression.

Although such a pattern is most recognisable if you are clinically depressed, its fingerprints are everywhere. In fact, the same 'cutting off' from enjoyment happens whenever we are driven and over-busy. It's an entirely natural feature of the human mind and arises out of its fine-tuned mechanism for focusing on complex tasks – an amazing ability, and one that's at a premium in our increasingly fast-paced world. And it happens because one of the ways that the mind focuses on one goal is by simply damping down the attractiveness of the alternatives.

A good example is when you are studying for an exam, or towards any important task or deadline, and you feel compelled to cut out all distractions. When engrossed, you may skip meals as your concentration suppresses your hunger. You stop seeing friends, family and acquaintances, while becoming less interested in hobbies and the myriad other fun little things that you usually enjoy. This isn't so much because you are focusing on the task at hand, but rather, your mind is squeezing out the alternatives by making them seem less enticing. In fact, the more attractive they used to be, the more they need to be dampened. It's like a selective depression. Everything but the main task becomes depressed, making it shine like a beacon in the wilderness. In the short term, this is a highly effective strategy. The problem arises when the project is finished. Even after the stress has gone and your energy has returned, it can be hard to get the zest back into life. Not only do you feel exhausted, but the things that you suppressed are no longer enjoyable. The suppression has done its job a little too well. Sometimes, even merely *thinking* about the things you used to enjoy can make you feel worse, like you are 'unworthy' in some way. They have become signals that life has no purpose, isn't much fun any more, that it's just one long slog after another.

If this continues, it can lead to clinical depression – and other mental-health problems, too. Such problems can then become embedded when the mind tries to work out *why* you have become so unhappy, stressed, anxious and exhausted. It takes on the all-consuming project of sorting out 'me'. It focuses all its resources on trying to answer such questions as 'Why am I such a failure?' 'Why can't I enjoy anything?' 'Why don't I have any *real* friends?' as you become increasingly preoccupied by them. They command attention. Then, just as with other major projects, the mind's natural tendency kicks in, inhibiting and suppressing everything else as it focuses, absolutely and completely, on sorting itself out, while your capacity for enjoyment simply evaporates. So depression and other mental-health problems aren't 'mistakes'. You haven't done anything wrong; you are not weak or a failure. You are simply a person with a mind that is doing its best in the only way it knows how.

Even just getting through daily life can produce similar effects. Everyday activities often need lots of juggling, so you suppress one thing while you get on with another. And it's seemingly endless, with a relentless pace and never enough time available. Procrastination is very common – waiting for 'the right time' or 'the right frame of mind' to do a task, only to make the painful discovery that the 'right time' never comes.[1] Most of us do this a little bit pretty much all the time. And here's the thing: research has found that each time we procrastinate, the act of suppression or 'pushing away' ensures that the postponed activity shifts further towards the more unpleasant end of the feeling-tone spectrum.[2] The task itself doesn't change, but it progressively acquires an unpleasant 'taste'. Then, the longer you put it off, the worse the taste becomes because you have pushed it away so often. And this happens through no fault of your own (nor of the poor task, which is just the same as before) but in your mind it has become ever more negative and harder to do. See box below.

Dealing with procrastination

We are all familiar with waiting for the 'right time' or the 'right frame of mind' to do something but then never actually getting around to doing it. Such procrastination is very common and can be extremely debilitating.[3] Joseph Ferrari and colleagues[4] have found that procrastination is even more common if you:

- overestimate how much time you have left to perform a task or underestimate how long it will take to complete
- overestimate how motivated you will be in the future

- mistakenly assume that you need to be in the 'right mood' or state of mind to work on a project
- believe that you work better under pressure, so it is best to leave everything till the last minute.

There are two main problems with these beliefs. Firstly, some tasks are not pleasant. Things such as putting out the rubbish or filling in a tax return are simply 'taking care of business', so if you wait for them to feel enjoyable, you will wait for a long time. Secondly, once you have ignored an activity for a little while, it acquires a so-called mental 'inhibition tag'. This means it may never be 'the right time' for you to actually do the task. In fact, the longer a task is delayed, the more entrenched this inhibition becomes. The mind's predictive model starts to give you a sense that it will be far more unpleasant than it really is. This can be reinforced by objective reality (returning library books where the fine becomes larger as time passes is a good example), but often it arises out of our own psychological processes.

Do you recall Chapter Two, where we described the origin of feeling tones? The need to discriminate between pleasant and unpleasant has been around since single-celled creatures learned to move towards sources of nourishment and safety and away from toxins and danger. Pleasantness and unpleasantness are associated with moving towards or away from such things. But it works the other way around, too. If we push something away, it acquires a sense of unpleasantness. Routine, unpleasant or inherently dull tasks can fall foul of this process. This is because we delay them in favour of more enjoyable things or perhaps tasks with a higher immediate priority. Such 'pushing away' ensures they become even more unpleasant and aversive. They may not have changed at all in themselves but have simply acquired an unpleasant 'taste'. And the longer we put them off, the worse this taste becomes – because each 'pushing away' ratchets up the feelings of unpleasantness and aversion.

It can be even worse than this if you are very distractible or experiencing emotional difficulties, such as depression. These not only make you doubt your abilities and set a very high standard for success, but they also give you a huge project to work on (sorting out your problems). And as we've seen, this makes the mind inhibit everything else.

As previously mentioned, procrastination is common, so there is no need to worry if it happens to you occasionally, but if it starts to bother you, remember that you can use this week's practices to explore what lifts you and what weighs you down and help you to choose the balance of activities you would like to have in your everyday life. You will gain the information and insights you need to choose a few activities that are simply enjoyable and others that, however small, will help you take care of business.

In time, you may learn to recognise the early warning signs of procrastination, and gently explore what it is like to turn towards the very task that was about to be delayed, noticing what's happening in your body as you do. You may discover that both the inherently enjoyable activities and the 'taking-care-of-business' tasks are also taking care of you.

As the procrastination process continues, more and more things acquire an unpleasant taste. Eventually, all that is left is that horrible feeling of life trickling through your fingers. When this happens – when life has lost its colour and you feel lost, alone or rudderless – attempting to return to what you enjoyed in the past, all at once, may not be helpful. It's the equivalent of expecting Tabby the cat to eat at the place she found terrifying. What you need is a way of rediscovering life's little pleasures using a step-by-step approach, similar to the one that helped Tabby. And that is the aim of this week: to gradually reinvigorate your life by rediscovering those things that lift your spirits, and then gradually tiptoe towards them. It will help you to take your first steps back to your life's favourite corner with its metaphorical saucer of milk.

Practices for Week Seven

- **Reflection Meditation** – should be carried out on six days out of seven (meditation 7.1). Once you are familiar with the practice, use the minimal instructions (Mi) version (7.2).
- **In addition to the Reflection Meditation, practise any of the previous meditations from this course** on six days out of seven for either twenty minutes once a day or ten minutes twice a day. You can practise the same one every day or a different one. Perhaps you might choose to use a Week One meditation on Day One, a Week Two meditation on Day Two and so on through the six days of your practice week. If you do this, feel free to use the Mi version of each one. On at least one day this week, practise for thirty minutes.

- **Two Everyday Mindfulness practices: Action Choices and Mindful Speaking and Listening.** The Action Choices practice (page 226) is for when you feel the need to take a pause in the midst of a busy day. Mindful Speaking and Listening (meditation 7.3) prepares you for when you are with others and wish to engage with them more effectively.

All meditations for this week can be found at littlebrown.co.uk/deeper-mindfulness/week-7

The meditations can also be found on the authors' website at franticworld.com/deeper-mindfulness

LIFTING FRAYED SPIRITS

Before you start the main meditation practices, there is a short two-step activity that asks you to reflect on the things that lift your spirits and those that sap them. You might like to try it now, rather than putting it off until later.

Step One: Rediscovering life's little pleasures

In the first column of the box below or in your journal, write a list of the things that you used to enjoy when life felt better, when it was less busy or before you became low or exhausted. They might be hobbies, pastimes or interests from a long time ago – maybe from your childhood, teens or twenties. They might be big or small; anything from stomping in muddy puddles to going to festivals or eating in a favourite restaurant and drinking a good wine or local homebrew. The list can be in any order at all. Take a moment, right now, to bring them to mind and write them down. You need not show the list to anyone else, so you can be open and honest with yourself. If you fill up the first column, continue on another sheet of paper. In the second column, rate each activity on the list on a scale from one to ten for how much enjoyment it used to bring. In the third column, rate each one on a scale from zero to minus ten for how much *effort* you feel it would take to do it right now (with minus ten being the most difficult).

I used to enjoy	Enjoyed 1 to 10	Effort 0 to −10

Many people discover that the activities that they used to find the most enjoyable now feel the most difficult. They have turned negative in proportion to how positive they felt before. Often, there is no rhyme or reason why something on the list should feel so hard. It just does. If this is the case, there is nothing wrong with you. It is exactly what we would expect. Your mind has tried to cope with your circumstances but has done so in a way that feels upsetting and painful: it has suppressed those activities that might have distracted you most because you found them enjoyable. These insights are invaluable because you can use them to chart a path back towards a happier and more fulfilling life. You can make a start on this by drawing up a different list, one with the easiest activities at the start – those that you can do now, or at least contemplate doing. At the end of the list will be items that either feel too difficult to do or you simply cannot imagine getting much pleasure from them at the moment. Draw up this list now, using the box below, and also write down the first step that you will take.

Re-engaging with activities I used to enjoy	
Easiest	First step?

Re-engaging with activities I used to enjoy	

Once you have drawn up the second list, you might like to try re-engaging with some of the activities, starting with the things that feel easiest. Take your time. You don't have to do all of them, or indeed any of them, and certainly not today (unless you wish to). We are being deliberately non-prescriptive here. Your decisions should be entirely personal and tailored to how you feel. You can use the Action Choices practice (overleaf) to help with this. This invites you to take brief pauses during the day to tune in to your mind's and body's 'weather pattern'. It is especially useful in those moments when you move from one activity to another. These are the moments when you can be easily swayed by your prevailing mood or hijacked by procrastination. The Action Choices practice will help you to sense the things that lighten your spirits but which are normally missed as you rush through the day. In this way, the practice will help you to choose the items on this list you should do, *when* you should do them and for how long. So it will help you to begin rebalancing your life.

Everyday Mindfulness Practice: Action Choices

In the next few hours of your day, see how many times a natural break occurs, or whether there's a moment when you finish one activity and start another. See if it's possible to use these moments to take a mindful pause; it may be a breath, or few breaths or many breaths. However long or short, take the opportunity to tune in to the weather pattern in body and mind at that moment. Ask yourself: 'Is this what I had intended to be doing right now?', and then, in that very moment, make a choice, before resuming the activities of your day.

Although simple, this practice is more significant than you might expect. Psychologists Mukul Bhalla and Dennis Proffitt[5] asked volunteers to estimate the steepness of hills. Some of them were asked to carry a heavy backpack, others carried no such bag. They found that carrying the backpack increased the perceived steepness of the hill. A similar overestimation of steepness was found in runners who evaluated the hill before and after an exhausting run. When tired, the runners overestimated its steepness. Unsurprisingly, when they did the same experiment with volunteers of different ages, the older participants thought the hill was steeper.

This close association between your physiological state and perception is profoundly significant. Low mood creates the bodily states that affect how you see the world; hills look steeper than they are, roads look longer and, as you'll know if you've ever had young children in the back of a car, time seems to drag on for ever. For these reasons, it is important to repeatedly 'check in' with yourself as you move through your day.

The Action Choices practice can become a personal 'reality check' of great long-term importance. With this in mind, if you are feeling tired or otherwise low or deflated, your prediction of how difficult or enjoyable an activity will be is likely to be biased towards the negative. And it will change from day to day, so it is worth carrying out this exercise more than once.

Step Two: Life's a balloon

Think of a hot-air balloon floating gently upwards as it begins a long journey.[6] Imagine that the balloon itself represents the lift and energy you feel when happy, healthy and in control of your life. And let the basket beneath the balloon represent the heaviness you feel when 'depleted'; those times when you feel the need to withdraw from the world. You might like to see the balloon's movement through the air as embodying the way that your experience changes from moment to moment – the way that small events can compound to make significant differences over time.

Thinking back to the last few days, go through a typical one and make a mental note of the ordinary things that you do. These might include taking a shower, eating breakfast, meeting a friend for a drink, commuting to work, chatting to colleagues or grabbing a sandwich at lunchtime. You can be as detailed as you like. If you spend much of your day apparently doing the same things, try breaking them down into smaller elements, such as updating a spreadsheet, checking email, moving stock around, or talking to clients. As you bring to mind each one in turn, see if you can feel their physical and emotional impact. Do they feel pleasant, unpleasant or somewhere in between? Repeat this exercise for a typical evening and weekend. When you have done so, look at the picture of the balloon (overleaf).

The balloon experiment: What lifts? What drags?

In each box of the balloon's canopy, write down one of the experiences that created a feeling of lift or energy as you brought it to mind. Feel free to add more boxes if there are not enough or make your own drawing in your journal and work with that. Try to remember that there are no right or wrong answers and each one is personal to you. For example, some people find it pleasant to cook or to spend time with their family while others do not. What 'lifts' you is what lifts *you*.

Once you have finished, reflect on what it is about these activities that creates the lift. If it isn't the activity itself, what is it? Perhaps it is the connection with certain people, pets or places; or maybe it arises out of taking care of yourself, meeting your basic needs or completing certain tasks; from a sense of success or achievement, being creative or expressive; or out of a feeling of strength, control or dexterity after doing what you love; or through simple movement or exercise. Spend a few moments reflecting on these ideas before moving on to the next stage.

When you feel ready, outside the balloon's basket, write down those things that weigh you down, deplete you of energy, make you feel tense, or otherwise distressed. Include things that make you feel less alive and present, as though you are merely existing rather than truly living. Spend a few moments reflecting on why you think each one creates these feelings. If it isn't the activity itself, what is it? Is it the connection with people, places, situations or scenarios? There might be several other interweaving factors, such as lack of control, choice or time. Are these factors the opposite of those that gave the balloon its lift? Or perhaps there is no connection at all? When you focus on them, how do you feel?

The aim of this exercise is not to shock you into making big decisions or into radically reforming your life, but to give you an indication of the balance between the things that lift your spirits and those that drag them down. The balance need not be perfect. One uplifting pastime can easily outweigh a long list of negative ones. It is also perfectly normal to spend some days with your spirits slowly sinking lower, while on others you are wafted towards the heavens. What matters is that you keep your life broadly in balance, so that your balloon maintains a generally stable altitude and doesn't crash land.

There are three ways you can stop your balloon from crashing: you can lessen the weight of the basket, inflate the balloon or, more realistically, try a combination of both.

Bearing all this in mind, what do you think might reduce the weight of the basket? Are you overworking or otherwise too busy? What else might reduce its weight? It might be a change in attitude towards those things that drag you down, or perhaps you can give them more time or space so you are less stressed or 'rushed' as you do them, or you might like to re-evaluate their significance and realise that some are simply not worth doing. As you re-evaluate your priorities, remember that the basket is more manageable if the balloon is well inflated. Have you inadvertently given up things that would normally 'lift' the balloon? You might also like to reflect on the list you drew up in Step One. As you do so, pay attention to your overall mood. How does it affect your choices? Are there some that you find especially hard to do when feeling down? You might like to leave these for a while. Are there others that feel easier to do that would, even now, this week, bring a sense of uplift? You might also like to bear in mind that often, when depressed or otherwise deflated, motivation follows some way behind the decision to begin. So you actually need to make a start before you will know for certain whether or not you will enjoy it.

And always remember that without lift, you, just like the balloon, are in danger of crash landing; it's called exhaustion but – again, like the balloon – a few short bursts of lift may be all that you need.

With this practice, we are once again being deliberately non-prescriptive. You now have the skills to 'fly solo' and make your own decisions. And the Reflection meditation (see box below) is designed to help you with this.

Remember, also, that each day you should do a meditation from one of the previous weeks of the course – you can do the same one each day or choose on an ad-hoc basis (see box page 221 earlier). You have the necessary skills, even though it might not always feel like it.

Reflection Meditation

What nourishes and what depletes ...

This is a reflection on what's happened over the past twenty-four hours – what you appreciate most, and what you appreciate least. Practising this regularly can help you meet each moment of the day with greater balance, insight and compassion.

Grounding

1. Finding a place to sit or lie down, bring attention to the sensations in the feet, the contact with seat, the hands or the breath. If you are focusing on the breath, notice the

in-breath and the out-breath and the spaces in between. Then at a certain point, expand your attention to the body as a whole, sitting or lying here.

Review of the past twenty-four hours

2. When you're ready, bring to mind the events of the past twenty-four hours: events large and small, important or trivial; people you've met; places you've been; journeys. What's been happening? If you stayed in one place, what things did you do and what did you notice?

What was appreciated most?

3. Ask yourself, 'What did I most appreciate in the day? What gave me energy? What did I find most nourishing?'

Creating more nourishment in your life

4. Then reflect on these questions: 'What might I do differently to build more nourishment into tomorrow?' 'What might I do to build in things that will lighten the load – things that I'd appreciate?'

   If nothing comes to mind, that's fine. You can reflect on this at some other time. Then, at a certain point, return to the sensations of the breath or some other place in the body, to ground yourself as you sit or lie here.

What was least appreciated?

5. And as you've been reviewing the day, you may have come across some moments that were more difficult. Ask yourself, 'What did I appreciate least in the day?' 'What made things heavier for me?' 'What took *away* energy?' Allow this moment to come to mind if you choose. Allow it to remain for a few moments, noticing any reactions to it ... any thoughts, feelings or body sensations. Remember that you don't have to like these feelings; it's OK not to like them, not to want them around. See if it's possible to be open to them, to allow them to be as they are.

Dealing skilfully with such moments

6. Ask yourself, 'Next time such moments occur, how might I meet them more skilfully if I choose to?' Remember to be kind to yourself. If nothing comes to mind at this time, that's fine. Simply opening to the possibility of dealing differently with such things can begin to change patterns of the mind.

Ending

7. At a certain point, return to the breath in the body as you sit or lie here, and allow one of the things that you most appreciated to come to mind again – a sense of being nourished, having energy, being alive.

And when you're ready, bring the practice to a close.

A bath, a walk, a little quiet time for yourself, visiting a friend, listening to music, dancing alone or with a loved one, spending a little extra time shopping for healthy food while savouring its flavours and aromas. This week focuses on those little things that directly nourish your spirit, 'lift your balloon' and keep life in balance. It helps you to become aware of the simple pleasures that have drained away from your life, often without you realising it.

In Gemma's case, it was a relaxing end-of-day bath that had been missing from her life. 'It is such a small thing, but it always felt like a precious gift to myself,' she said. 'I'd compiled a list of things that were weighing down my balloon's basket, and those that inflated its canopy, and realised that my life was completely out of balance. In the short term, there wasn't much I could do about the big things that were weighing me down, so I started with the small things that I knew could lift my spirits. I started with a bath. Really, it was that simple. I'd get into the bath with all my muscles tensed up into knots and be full of worries and recriminations – with my inner critic warning me about the dangers of wasting my time in this way. It kept on telling me that I should take a quick shower instead and leave taking a bath until I had more time. And I nearly took its advice. Then I remembered the promise that I'd made to myself at the beginning of the course that, come what may, I would complete it and follow its instructions to the letter. I'd told myself that it was only eight weeks long, so I wouldn't lose much by at least trying. This was just the licence I needed to gently shoo away the inner critic and hop into the bath. And it was so gloriously magical to feel all my troubles melt away for half an hour. After a few daily baths, I started adding a couple of glittery bath bombs to the mix. I slept like a log afterwards, too!'

Giving yourself licence to be kind to yourself can be crucial, especially if you have been overly busy, or working too hard or the world feels like it's resting heavily on your shoulders. No matter how frivolous this week might seem, it is, in fact, central to the success of the whole programme. We can teach you the technicalities of mindfulness, but the real meditation is how you actually live your life. It reminds you that in the long run, life is short; that it's the succession of tiny moments that marks out a life well lived. And when you begin to sense this, it adds a certain clarity to life, that it must be truly lived and experienced, day by day. Procrastination can be an unseen barrier to this. It's unseen because it often creates a false sense that you are organising and optimising your life by prioritising tasks that are endlessly juggled and delayed as you wait for the perfect moment to do them – a moment that never quite arrives.

It's important to prevent procrastination from gaining a foothold and monopolising your time. For this reason, when you choose to do an activity – whether for pleasure or to 'take care of business' – it will help if you make a specific time for it in your diary, rather than allowing it to be a general intention. See if it's possible to take into account your other priorities and deadlines, so that you're not forced to reorganise things again at the last minute. When you do this, you may discover that you have simply taken on too many tasks. If this is the case, you may need to reassess your priorities and delay some things and decline to do others. If something seems too large to do all at once, then break it down into smaller steps. For example, clearing out a single drawer, rather than a whole chest of drawers; working on a section of an essay rather than the whole thing; or responding to one email rather than to all the messages in your inbox. If you are depressed, take special care by limiting the time spent on a task. Ten minutes may be all that you can manage, but even making a start will bring huge relief. But even if you are not depressed, set a timer to remind yourself to take a break every thirty to forty-five minutes. If you are feeling exhausted, you may have got into the habit of staying up late and dropped an hour or two of sleep as a result. If you can, you might catch up during the course of this week by either taking a nap or two during the day (each for less than half an hour) or going to bed earlier, having put your phone out of reach. It is astonishing how corrosive a lack of sleep can be. And often, you are only aware of its negative effects once you've caught up and look back at previous days.

Everyday Mindfulness Practice: Speaking and Listening

If you wish to bring mindfulness into every area of your life, one of the best ways is to cultivate mindfulness of speaking and listening. This is because most of us spend a great deal of our time in conversation.

At some point in the next few hours or the next chance you get, see if it's possible to bring attention to those moments when you are in conversation – at work, at home or as you move around your city, town or village.

When you are listening, see if it's possible to listen wholeheartedly without agreeing or disagreeing, or planning what you will say when it is your turn.

When you are speaking, ask yourself, how much of it is really necessary?

This is especially hard when you are speaking with someone about a third person who isn't present. Of course, it is sometimes necessary to speak about a third person who is not there, but it may be helpful sometimes to imagine that they could hear what you say. Would they recognise from the tone of what you say that they are loved and cared for or would they have heard only bitterness and exclusion. Is what you say truthful? And even if it is truthful, is it necessary, and if it feels necessary, is it kind? See if it's possible, in all your conversations, to say just what you need to say without overstating anything, and then stopping and listening.

In all of this, you are cultivating mindfulness within the very warp and weft of everyday life, and in doing so, you are learning how to live out a life of deep wisdom and compassion – a life full of kindness to yourself and to others.

As she did the balloon exercise, Frankie had an important insight that she needed to 'season her day'.

'I realised how I had neglected those activities that I find nurturing and how attitudes of graciousness, kindness and letting go promote a greater sense of contentment. In looking at what depletes me, my immediate response was "external factors", such as social media and the daily news. But looking more closely, I discovered that it was the brooding about things that I can't change, or the things that annoy me, that really drained the life out of me. And these found a route into my life through the media.'

Frankie decided to take a break from both social media and

the news: 'I'm a bit of news addict. I used to work in news-papers, so I adore its insanely fast pace. I genuinely love it; but I've also come to realise that it can give you a pretty jaundiced view of humanity. I've learned that if it's in the news, then it's vanishingly unlikely to happen to you – it's generally in the news precisely because it's unusual and doesn't happen very often. I've also learned that if a headline ends with a question mark, then the answer is usually "No". Think of tabloid headlines like: "Is your parrot psychic?" I *do* know all this, but I was still getting drawn in. My willpower simply wasn't strong enough to resist, so I put myself on a very strict "media diet" of avoiding everything for one week. I was especially strict with social media. They have algorithms to get you addicted – genuinely psychologically addicted – so this was especially hard.'

Frankie then discovered that there was a void in the centre of her life where the social media used to be. So she decided to 'season her day' with the Action Choices practice: little pauses in which she could ground herself, appreciate her life and give gratitude to those around her. So instead of snacking on social media, she feasted on her life as it was happening. And as with seasoning, you don't need a lot of it to make a big difference.

Frankie then decided to meet up with a good friend she hadn't seen for ages. 'I realised just how much I'd missed her,' she said. 'How nice it was. And I also realised that *who* you meet also matters. This is where the Speaking and Listening meditation really helped. It would have been easy to slip into our old habits of talking and listening from our shared past, but instead I decided to dig deep into how her life had changed in the three years since I'd last seen her. So I kind of got to re-know her all over again. The same good friend but with lots of juicy new experiences to tell me about. Soon though, we got into gossiping about someone we both knew, but then I got a feeling that it wouldn't make either of us feel good to go there, so I was silent for a while, then we laughed about some other things from our past and we had a good time.'

Emma, too, noticed a profound change in heart and mind this week. Her life had seemed to be spinning out of control and the week-by-week feeling-tone practices had, she admitted, been hard to sustain. But with the help of her meditation teacher, she had persisted, moving in and out without judgment. Then, just as it seemed as if the struggle would go on for ever, something changed. She wrote in her diary:

Around Day Three, something shifted. It's not just in the way that I'm thinking – not just cognitive. It is something deep within me, a spaciousness ... a deep knowing that I will be OK. A shift in how I look at my circumstances. How I look at all the rushing and all the chaos. A shift in how I handle the resistance. I am still exhausted. But it feels less sticky, less constricted ... lighter and more restful. It feels as if something has created enough space for everything to be in there. Just saying, 'It's OK not to like this' has given permission for the bad stuff – and the good stuff – to be there. I'm no longer in constant struggle with the bad things in my life, while clinging and craving for the good things to remain. It's taught me to stop running away from my life. I think that might be what the shift actually is – a staying with, a release, a letting go. I know that this might sound fluffy, but it is so much better than feeling trapped and entangled by life. Now I know that I will be OK whatever life throws at me.

CHAPTER TWELVE

Week Eight: The Adventure Continues

Vedana is the oft-forgotten element of mindfulness. Although truly foundational, it is frequently glossed over by mindfulness courses, partly because it can appear slightly enigmatic – too subtle, perhaps – to easily fit into the modern world, but also because there is only so much that can be meaningfully taught on an eight-week programme. The latest developments in neuroscience changes all this. It turns out, feeling tones are central to the way that we make sense of the world and to how, occasionally, we can become entangled in suffering. So rather than remaining on the periphery of mindfulness, it can now be welcomed centre stage. And this accords with the earliest traditions that gave rise to mindfulness. Quite amazingly, ideas and practices that are at least 2,500 years old can help us to find the peace necessary to thrive in the twenty-first century. Vedana brings meditation into our post-modern world – where it not only fits but truly belongs.

It is often said that the real meditation is how you live your life. This is especially so for vedana because it helps you to live consciously and with *intent*, so that your life becomes your meditation and meditation your life. Conscious intent allows us to pierce the veils that separate us from the world as it truly is – a world that is often far more subtle, changeable and beautiful than we imagine. It allows us to calm our storms before they overwhelm us and to act out of wisdom rather than raw, reactive emotion. You now have the skills necessary to do all of this. Although there is still much to learn, we cannot teach you much more. Soon, you will need to become your own teacher and guide yourself. That's what this chapter is designed to do. Here, we'll help you to consolidate all that you have learned so far and ready you for your journey. But first, it will be helpful to see how far you have come, and then you can decide how (or even if) you wish to build vedana into the rest of your life.

Moving fluently through the world demands that the brain make continuous predictions about what you are about to see, hear, taste, smell and touch. These are updated every moment by incoming sensory data, but if no differences from your prediction are found, what you experience is the *prediction* made inside your head, not the data from outside of it. This is based on sensory data stored in a short-term cache – or super-fast memory. Feeling tones, too, are a fundamental aspect of these predictions; both data and feeling tones are inextricably entwined in the cache. This is why we live inside our heads so often. It's the default option.

It's no wonder, then, that you are thrown again and again into old habits of emotional thinking – because the most intense of these feeling tones (the most unpleasant) seem to have the most urgent need for action. They are effortlessly served up by your mind's cache. Without precise data to update your simulation, you are compelled to live inside your mental models, gradually forgetting how to inhabit your actual life – how to engage directly with the experience of being alive.

There is a further twist. Depending on where such feeling tones fall on the spectrum, from pleasant to unpleasant, the direction of our action and its urgency is determined. If this feeling tone is *not* clearly seen, it presses our buttons. Left to itself, it automatically creates a pulse of reactivity. This reactivity pulse might include resistance against what we don't like, pursuit of what we do like or, sometimes, a dampening of the positive to avoid disappointment. Such feeling tones are easily missed and yet they are the very tipping points that can do so much damage to us and our relationships. You know how the next bit of the story goes – automatic reactivity can set in motion a whole cascade of thoughts, feelings, sensations, images and emotions. It's like a photo burst (a fast succession of images), sliding effortlessly from real-world data, which can be bad enough, and on to fabrication, which is even worse. And all the while, the body is readying itself for action based on the worst imaginings of this photo burst. Frame by frame, our bodies are preparing to react to every worst-case scenario. This then feeds back into our predictions because we understand the world through action. Every thought, feeling, emotion and sensation – indeed, everything that we are capable of experiencing – is reflected and understood through the corresponding actions played out in the mind and body. No wonder we so often feel stressed and exhausted.

Although we can't do anything about the underlying vedana, we can slow things down and look at them frame by frame. We can use these moments to dissolve the link between the feeling tone and the reactivity pulse that would have followed. And, over time, a long and vicious cycle can be gently transformed into a virtuous one.

In Week One of the course, you learned how to find *firm ground*, so that your mind was no longer blown about by the inevitable distractions of everyday life. You learned that the breath could be a wonderful place to ground your attention, but also that there are alternative points of focus available to you: the sensations of contact between your feet and the floor, between your body and what you are sitting or lying on and between your hands and your lap or your thighs.

In Week Two, you learned that when your mind wanders during meditation, there is an alternative to immediately forcing your mind to refocus its awareness on your chosen subject. Even if you have been practising mindfulness for a long time, you may have a touch of frustration when your mind wanders. You feel you should be better at this by now. You may look enviously at other meditators, or images in the media, or at mindfulness teachers, and believe that they have perfected meditation. Such serenity! You then compare what *you* feel like on the *inside* with what *they* look like on the *outside*. This can be toxic. So instead, you practised relating to your own mind with a sense of gratitude and wonder, making every occasion of mind-wandering an opportunity to see it from a new, wider and kinder perspective. This changes everything; more mind-wandering means more gratitude, more affection towards this most intimate part of who you are. And you also practised bringing your everyday senses into the centre stage of awareness. Little by little, you saw how each sense door brings not only sensations but also a *feel* of those sensations, a gut-level read-out of pleasantness, unpleasantness or some-where in between.

In Week Three, you built on this by noticing that thoughts, and even whole streams of thoughts, as well as the emotions that come with them, arise entangled with feeling tones. And there's something remarkable about this discovery. There is a lot going on in mind and body. Thoughts, sensations and emotions are complex, and we can easily get over-analytical about them, tying ourselves in knots trying to unravel and understand their 'true' significance. But with feeling tone, there are but three aspects: pleasant, unpleasant and neutral. Nothing else. Simply acknow-ledging this purity is liberating. And so, during Week Three, you practised becoming more attuned to the subtlety of such feeling tones without judgment or analysis.

You built on this skill during Week Four by simply allowing things to be as they are. Gently saying to yourself, 'It's OK not to like this' or, 'It's OK to like this' was a reminder that your body and mind are a part of nature and your reactions are natural and entirely normal. And by intentionally practising gratitude, you saw how we all have a natural and pervasive bias towards the unpleasant. This creates a 'blanket of indifference' that we throw over many small pleasures that might otherwise nourish our spirits. But often we don't even notice them, which is astonishing, but equally astonishing is the discovery that they are still there, waiting for us to rediscover them, like long-lost friends we've neglected, but who are none the less delighted to see us again.

Week Five returned to the central new discovery from psy-chology and neuroscience: that actions do not arise as the final stage of an elaborate process of perception and the processing of raw data from the world. Actions are, instead, central to how you understand the world at the very first moment of perception. To perceive what's going on around you, you first need to simulate and rehearse an action. You cannot even understand what someone is saying to you, think a thought, remember the past or make a plan, without the brain rehearsing the corresponding actions. It's almost as if troops are being mobilised; readying for battle, practising their manoeuvres and carrying out 'live-fire' exercises – and doing so for every thought, feeling, sensation and emotion that arises every moment of every day. No wonder you often feel so exhausted! So we explored the benefits of saying gently to yourself, 'No action needed right now.' This wasn't to stop you responding wisely. On the contrary, it is simply that most of the brain's busyness when it prepares for action is irrelevant. And certainly, when you are in the middle of a meditation, action is not generally necessary. So 'No action needed right now' brings its own relief. The troops stand down, there is a sense of rest, of peace. And this serenity carries over into the rest of your day and helps you to realise that often – quite often – no action is the wisest course of action.

In Week Six, you gathered together all these new skills and began turning towards your difficult emotions. You practised the skill of befriending yourself and allowing difficult emotions to be present in mind and heart. You saw where in the body they revealed themselves and then acknowledged each one's feeling tone by saying, 'It's OK not to like this' if it was unpleasant and then quietly adding, 'No action needed right now.' So there was a sense of making space for the difficulty as it occurred in the body, not trying to push it away; for such pushing away actually makes it worse – makes it seem even more unpleasant.

In Week Seven, you explored how, when you become tired or preoccupied, you lose contact with those little things that nourish your soul and make life worth living. They slip out of your life, leaving behind only the things that sap your spirits and erode your quality of life. But it can be even worse than this – because when you feel low, even *thinking* of those things that used to bring pleasure can trigger aversion. So you want to push them away – and you simply cannot imagine them ever being pleasant again. Simply recognising this, and not blaming yourself for it is really quite cathartic. You can then explore the possibility of reclaiming your life, little by little, using daily practices of noticing small beauties and pleasures that you may have taken for granted.

And now, here you are at Week Eight, with the opportunity to reflect on what has happened to you, what difficulties, delights and discoveries you have made through the programme. And you can decide what you would like to take forwards with you into the future. So take a moment to sit in your meditation space and reflect on the following questions. Take your time.

- What did you wish for while doing the programme in this book?
- What have you learned?
- What have been the difficulties and challenges for you?
- How have you worked with them?

Then, when you are ready – for there is no rush – take a further moment to sit, focusing on your breath and body, perhaps listening to the Finding Your Ground meditation, and reflect on these questions:

- Is there more you'd like to explore?
- What might hinder you and how will you work with this?
- What will support you most effectively?

At this point, you might feel both excited and daunted: excited by the further potential of vedana, but daunted by the choices you feel you will need to make. After all, where should you begin and what will give you the most effective support?

Many people have found that regularity, structure and momentum are important in maintaining a meditation practice. So, first, decide how much time you are willing and able to realistically dedicate to your practice each day. Try not to overestimate this, but equally, you will need to make a certain minimum commitment. Meditating for twenty to thirty minutes a day on five to six days each week is ideal. If you can't do this, then even ten minutes a day will suffice. Mindfulness is a lifelong endeavour, and its benefits accrue over months and years, so regularity is more important than bingeing, then crashing and bingeing again.

And what should you practise? The practices themselves will teach you. Some days, you will feel the need to ground yourself with the Finding Your Ground meditation. On others, you might need to remind yourself that there is 'No action needed right now' with the Feeling-tone Moment by Moment practice. Still, it will be helpful to have a structure to work from, and on page 253, you'll find some suggestions for practising month by month for a whole year. These are only ideas based on our experience of what has helped others. Many of our students have found it helpful to do a practice with the same theme or intention for longer than just one week. So we recommend staying with the same set of practices for a month. This commitment does two things. Firstly, it means you don't have to start your practice each day by deciding what to do. Having to decide can put pressure on you and trigger procrastination. It can also take time away from the practice itself. Secondly, day-by-day repetition allows you to see the changes that each day brings. These changes can be subtle or significant and may be due to all sorts of different causes and conditions, such as the weather outside or the 'weather inside' your mind and body – what you did earlier in the day or on previous days, the people you met, the joys and sorrows you encountered or the projects you felt trapped by and those that you completed. Such day-to-day changes can be seen more clearly if your practice remains stable for a longer period.

Feel free to use the tracks from the programme – either the guided meditations or the Mi versions. Use the timing track with bells when you wish to guide yourself. However, don't feel compelled to guide yourself. Both of us still use guided-meditation tracks from time to time. It can also be very therapeutic to be on a 'mini home retreat' and to spend time being led through meditations.

As you attempt the meditations, you might find yourself putting them off. You might recognise it as procrastination. If this is the case, try to remember the advice of yoga teachers: 'The hardest move in yoga is the move on to your mat.' And if this doesn't reassure you, you might promise yourself to do a meditation practice for just one minute. Yes, just one minute. And if after one minute you decide to continue, simply carry on to the end of the track.

Remember earlier in this chapter when we mentioned that vedana was often only discussed briefly during conventional mindfulness courses because there is only so much that can be taught during an eight-week programme? We have faced the same dilemma with this course. There is one element that we needed to miss out because it is not central to this vedana course but that will, none the less, be very rewarding. We call them Habit Releasers. These are designed to gently loosen the bonds that habits hold over you. They are short and enjoyable practices that will bring you great benefits if you pay attention to your feeling tone as you do them. In this way, they are little catalysts that will help to embed the benefits of your meditations. You'll find a list of them in the box below. Try focusing on one or two each month.

Habit Releasers

Choose any one or two of the following each month and explore what it's like to do them as an experiment, noting its feeling tone:

- Wherever you walk this month, outside or inside, make it 5 per cent slower.
- As you are walking or commuting, whoever you see, silently wish them well, perhaps by saying inwardly 'May you be well', knowing that they have the same longing as you to be happy, relaxed and to live a life free from suffering.
- Put your smartphone out of reach when watching TV, working or when it's on charge overnight. If a smartphone is in view it can decrease concentration and performance by 20 per cent[1]).

- Go 'unplugged' for one day each week this month: so no email, no web browsing, no computer or phone (if possible).
- Limit answering emails to half an hour at a time this month (or decide in advance for how long). Set a timer and practise obeying it.
- Put your own name in your calendar for an hour's appointment once a week this month, and do whatever you want – absolutely anything, big, small or even nothing at all.
- Put a signature on your email that includes a message that says that you do not generally answer mail between 7pm and 7am.
- Schedule a long-forgotten pleasant activity (listening to music, reading a favourite poem, visiting somewhere you long for).
- Schedule something you've been putting off, no matter how small.
- Write a card to someone you used to know with whom you've been out of contact.
- Practise saying 'No' this month to new commitments that would interfere with things you have already committed to.
- Choose a skill that you once wanted to have (for example, playing the guitar, pottery making, drawing, or a sport) and take the first steps towards learning it. Being open to new ideas such as learning a new skill is one of the five factors of wellbeing.
- You will find a more comprehensive list of Habit Releasers at franticworld.com/releasers

WARNING SIGNS OF EMOTIONAL TURBULENCE OR FATIGUE

There will be times when you feel overwhelmed. Your practice may falter. You may feel lost and alone. You will feel as if you are sliding backwards, never to regain the glimpses of progress you had seen.

Life can be very hard indeed. Crippling, sometimes.

How will you recognise such times? It will not be obvious because they will arrive with their own compelling propaganda stream. Here are some indications (but remember that the stories you tell yourself will be as unique as you are): you may go quiet or bang doors or drawers; your sleep may become disturbed or you may sleep too much; exhaustion and fatigue are very common; the things that you used to enjoy start to lose their lustre. Here is another hint: look out for thoughts or speech that include 'absolutes'. These are words such as *always, never, no one, everyone, nothing, totally, entire, everything.* This sort of language is a more reliable sign of emotional distress than negative words.[2] It is a warning that you are close to stress, exhaustion and depression, signalling that it is time to be very gentle with yourself; time to look for ways of nourishing yourself and to keep a cool head as you decide what is the most effective course of action.

The ability to stand back – even if for just one moment – to see the bigger picture – is what mindfulness of feeling tones can help you with. Psychologists call this 'decentring' or 'disidentifying' and it is the route through which many therapies exert their most powerful effects.[3]

How can you decentre when all of life is pulling you inwards and binding you with chains?

Take one breath. Yes, just one breath . . .

Focus on wherever in your body the feelings are to be found . . .

Pleasant, unpleasant, neutral . . .

If unpleasant, gently remind yourself that 'It's OK not to like this.' 'No action needed right now.'

And then, as you relax into the quietness of your heart, and the moment begins to feel right, you can take a single, tiny, step forward.

A YEAR OF PRACTICE

The following month-by-month practices are suggestions only and encompass broad themes, so that you can guide your own meditations. Still, it is perfectly fine and quite normal to use – or return to – the fully guided practices should your energy or enthusiasm wane temporarily.

Month One

Grounding meditation then shifting your attention to your feet, contact with seat, hands and breath. (You can do this for either one week on each anchor or stay with just one or two for the whole month.) You can use meditations 1.2 and 1.4 if you wish.

Month Two

Brief grounding meditation, then mindfulness of the whole body. If the mind wanders, pause and cultivate gratitude for the mind (meditations 2.2 and 2.4). Practise the Finding Your Ground When You First Wake Up meditation at least once a week (1.6).

Month Three

Brief grounding meditation on breath or body then move on to mindfulness of sounds, then thoughts and on to feelings. Notice the tonality of whatever arises in mind and body (meditations 3.2 and 3.4). Practise Noticing the Feeling Tone in Everyday Life at least once a week (meditation 5.5).

Month Four

Walking meditations 4.2 and 4.4, with your attention focused on your feet, legs, whole body and the space around you (one week dedicated to each, if you prefer). Or use mindful stretching (meditation 4.5). When you notice a sensation or thought as pleasant or unpleasant, remind yourself, 'It's OK to like/not to like this.' Do the Ten-finger Gratitude practice (4.6) or the Everyday Mindfulness practice of Appreciation (4.8) at least once a week.

Month Five

Grounding meditation focused on your breath or body, moving on to mindfulness of sounds, then on to thoughts and feelings. End with open awareness, allowing all that arises in your consciousness to be held gently and with kindness. Notice the tonality of the body and mind on each out-breath, while gently reminding yourself, 'It's OK to like/not to like this' and, 'No action needed right now' (meditations 5.2 and 5.4). Practise Noticing the Feeling Tone in Everyday Life (5.5) at least once a week.

Month Six

Week 1:   Kindness practice (meditation 6.1)

Week 2:   Finding Your Ground meditation (as in
                 Month One: meditations 1.2 and 1.4)

Week 3:   Exploring Difficulty meditation (6.4)

Week 4:   Finding Your Ground meditations
                 (1.2 and 1.4)

Practise Turning Towards Difficulty at least once a week (meditation 6.6).

Month Seven

Grounding meditation focused on the breath or body, then move on to mindfulness of sounds, then thoughts and feelings. End with open awareness without a specific focus and notice the tonality of whatever arises in the mind and body, while saying to yourself, 'It's OK to like/not to like this' and, 'No action needed right now' (meditations 5.2 and 5.4).

Practise the Reflection meditation (7.1 or 7.2) at least once a week.

Month Eight

Grounding meditation focused on the feet, contact with the seat, hands and breath. Then stay with one anchor for the whole of each week or with just one or two throughout the whole month (meditations 1.2 and 1.4).

Practise Noticing the Feeling Tone in Everyday Life at least once a week (meditation 5.5).

Month Nine

Week 1:   Kindness practice (meditation 6.1)
Weeks 2 and 3: Exploring Difficulty (meditation 6.4)
Week 4:   Finding Your Ground meditation
                      (1.2 and 1.4)

Practise Turning Towards Difficulty at least once a week (meditation 6.6).

Month Ten

Mindful Stretching (meditation 4.5) or Walking meditation 4.1 to 4.4. Briefly ground yourself, then practise mindfulness of the whole body in movement. Notice and name the feeling tones of your sensations and thoughts, then say to yourself, 'It's OK to like/not to like this' and, 'No action needed right now.'

Practise Mindful Speaking and Listening at least once a week (meditation 7.3).

Month Eleven

Grounding meditation focused on the breath or body, moving on to mindfulness of sounds, then thoughts and feelings. End with open awareness, allowing all that arises in your consciousness to be held gently and with kindness, and notice the tonality of whatever arises in the mind and body. Remind yourself: 'It's OK to like/not to like this' and 'No action needed right now' (meditations 5.2 and 5.4).

Practise Everyday Mindfulness: Action Choices at least once a week (see page 226).

Month Twelve

The Kindness meditation (6.1) is the default option this month. You should also do other practices that you have found helpful over the year or which you would like to explore more fully.

Practise the Reflection meditation at least once a week (meditations 7.1 or 7.2).

RESOURCES

BOOKS

Mindfulness Self-Help Guides

Williams, M., & Penman, D., *Mindfulness: A Practical Guide to Finding Peace in a Frantic World* (London, Piatkus 2011). Published in US as *Mindfulness: An Eight-Week Plan for Finding Peace in a Frantic World* (Rodale, 2011).

Williams, J. M. G., Teasdale, J. D., Segal, Z. V. & Kabat-Zinn, J., *The Mindful Way Through Depression: Freeing Yourself from Chronic Unhappiness* (Guilford Press, 2007).

Teasdale, J. D., Williams, J. M. G. & Segal, Z. V., *The Mindful Way Workbook* (Guilford Press, 2013).

Penman, D., *The Art of Breathing: The secret to living mindfully. Just don't breathe a word of it . . .* (HQ, 2020). Published in US as *The Art of Breathing: How to Become at Peace with Yourself and the World* (Hampton Roads, 2022).

Pain and Chronic Illness

Burch, V. & Penman, D., *Mindfulness for Health: A Practical Guide to Relieving Pain, Reducing Stress and Restoring Wellbeing* (Piatkus, 2013). Published in US as *You Are Not Your Pain: Using Mindfulness to Relieve Pain, Reduce Stress, and Restore Well-Being: An Eight-Week Program* (Flatiron, 2015).

Creativity and Decision Making

Penman, D., *Mindfulness for a More Creative Life: Calm Your Busy Mind, Enhance Your Creativity and Find a Happier Way of Living* (Piatkus, 2021).

MBCT Manual For Therapists

Segal, Z. V., Williams, J. M. G. & Teasdale, J. D., *Mindfulness-Based Cognitive Therapy for Depression* (second edition, Guilford Press, 2013).

Emotions, Feelings and the Embodied Mind

Barrett L.F. *How Emotions Are Made: The Secret Life of the Brain* (Macmillan, 2017).

Damasio, A., *The Strange Order of Things: Life, Feeling and the Making of Cultures* (Penguin, 2017).

Clark, A., *Surfing Uncertainty: Prediction, Action and the Embodied Mind* (OUP, 2016).

WEBSITES

Mindfulness

www.franticworld.com

Our website to accompany this and our previous book. It contains a forum to discuss your experiences and to learn from others. There are links to further meditations and books that you might find useful, plus a section listing upcoming talks, events and retreats.

www.mbct.co.uk and www.oxfordmindfulness.org

Our Oxford-based websites: general introduction to MBCT: includes information on training.

https://www.oxfordmindfulness.org/learn-mindfulness/resources/

Meditation practices from Mindfulness-based Cognitive Therapy guided by Mark Williams.

www.bangor.ac.uk/mindfulness
Training in mindfulness-based approaches to healthcare, up to master's level, is offered at the University of Bangor, where Mark Williams was based before moving back to Oxford.

https://bamba.org.uk/
British Association of Mindfulness-based Approaches. An inclusive community of mindfulness practitioners, teachers, trainers and researchers.

www.mindfulnesscds.com
For tapes/CDs of meditation practices recorded by Jon Kabat-Zinn.

https://www.brown.edu/public-health/mindfulness/home
Mindfulness Centre at Brown University, Providence, Rhode Island

Buddhist Background

www.gaiahouse.co.uk
Gaia House, West Ogwell, Newton Abbot, Devon TQ12 6EW. A retreat centre in the insight meditation tradition (which is closest to the mindfulness practices taught in MBCT and MBSR).

www.dharma.org
Information about centres offering experience of the insight meditation tradition.

www.dharmaseed.org
Offers a large searchable library, updated regularly, of talks given (mostly on retreats) by teachers in the insight meditation tradition. Search for talks on *vedana* or *feeling tone* for talks explaining this foundational aspect of mindfulness practice.

LOOKING AFTER YOURSELF

If at any time you feel overwhelmed, do re-read the section in Chapter 5 (Week One). You don't have to 'grit your teeth' and meditate through an emotional storm. If overwhelming feelings persist, do reach out to friends or a mindfulness teacher, or talk to a family physician or a counsellor. If you find this route difficult, then look for resources and helplines that can assist. The Mental Health Foundation has good information: www.mentalhealth.org.uk – search for 'How to get help'. And the charity, Mind, has an information and signposting service – search for helpline in www.mind.org.uk. SANEline services is a helpline for those who have reached a crisis in their mental health www.sane.org.uk.

For information and discussion on the safety of mindfulness, see

http://oxfordmindfulness.org/news/is-mindfulness-safe/

AUSTRALIAN AND NEW ZEALAND RESOURCES

Meditation centres

www.dharma.org.au
Information about the centres that follow the insight meditation traditions (which are closest to the mindfulness practices taught in MBCT and MBSR) can often be found on this website.

Other online resources of interest

www.openground.com.au
For information on MBSR courses and training around Australia.

https://mindfulnessinaustralia.com/
Courses for practising and facilitating mindfulness in Australia.

www.canberramindfulnesscentre.com.au
MBSR courses and training in Canberra.

https://mindfulnessworksaustralia.com.au/
Provides introduction to mindfulness practice and further training across Australia.

https://mindfulnessworks.co.nz/
Provides introduction to mindfulness practice and further training across New Zealand.

AUDIO MEDITATIONS GUIDE

Here is a useful summary of the numbers and names of the meditations that feature in each week of the programme. All of the audio meditations can be found at littlebrown.co.uk/deeper-mindfulness or franticworld.com/deeper-mindfulness

WEEK ONE

Meditation 1.1:	10-minute Finding Your Ground meditation
Meditation 1.2:	20-minute Finding Your Ground meditation
Meditation 1.3:	30-minute Finding Your Ground meditation
Meditation 1.4:	Mi Finding Your Ground Meditation

| Meditation 1.5: | Sound of Bells only |
| Meditation 1.6: | Everyday Mindfulness Practice: Finding Your Ground When You First Wake – 3 minutes |

WEEK TWO

Meditation 2.1:	10-minute Taking a Pause meditation
Meditation 2.2:	20-minute Taking a Pause meditation
Meditation 2.3:	30-minute Taking a Pause meditation
Meditation 2.4:	Mi Taking a Pause meditation

Sound of Bells only

WEEK THREE

Meditation 3.1:	10-minute Feeling-tone meditation
Meditation 3.2:	20-minute Feeling-tone meditation
Meditation 3.3:	30-minute Feeling-tone meditation
Meditation 3.4:	Mi Feeling-tone meditation
Meditation 3.5:	Everyday Mindfulness Practice: End-of-day Reflection on Feeling Tone

Sound of Bells only

WEEK FOUR

Meditation 4.1:	10-minute Mindful Walking
Meditation 4.2:	20-minute Mindful Walking
Meditation 4.3:	30-minute Mindful Walking

Meditation 4.4:	Mi Mindful Walking
Meditation 4.5:	Mindful Stretches
Meditation 4.6:	Ten-finger Gratitude exercise
Meditation 4.7:	Mi Ten-finger Gratitude exercise
Meditation 4.8:	Everyday Mindfulness Practice: Appreciation
Meditation 4.9:	Resting when you can't sleep – 8 minutes

Sound of Bells only

WEEK FIVE

Meditation 5.1:	10-minute Feeling-tone Moment by Moment meditation
Meditation 5.2:	20-minute Feeling-tone Moment by Moment meditation
Meditation 5.3:	30-minute Feeling-tone Moment by Moment meditation
Meditation 5.4:	Mi Feeling-tone Moment by Moment meditation
Meditation 5.5:	Everyday Mindfulness Practice: Noticing the Feeling Tone in Everyday Life – 3 mins

Sound of Bells only

WEEK SIX

Meditation 6.1:	15-minute Kindness meditation
Meditation 6.2:	Mi Kindness meditation
Meditation 6.3:	10-minute Exploring Difficulty meditation

Meditation 6.4:   20-minute Exploring Difficulty meditation
Meditation 6.5:   Mi Exploring Difficulty meditation
Meditation 6.6:   Everyday Mindfulness Practice: Turning
                           Towards Difficulty

Sound of Bells only

WEEK SEVEN

Meditation 7.1:   Reflection meditation
Meditation 7.2:   Mi Reflection meditation
Meditation 7.3:   Everyday Mindfulness Practice:
                           Mindful Speaking and
                           Listening – 2½ mins

Key

Mi = Minimal instructions
Sound of Bells only: bell sounds every 5 minutes

REFERENCES

CHAPTER ONE

1. Adapted from pp. 19–20 *Into the Silent Land* by Martin Laird, with the kind permission of Martin Laird.
2. Segal, Z. V., Williams, J. M. G. & Teasdale, J. D., *Mindfulness-based Cognitive Therapy for Depression* (second edition, Guilford Press, 2013); Teasdale, J. D., Williams, J. M. G. & Segal, Z. V., *The Mindful Way Workbook: An Eight-Week Program to Free Yourself from Depression and Emotional Distress* (Guilford Press, 2014).
3. The Sanskrit word *vedana* was also used in Pali, a later language of the Indian sub-continent, and the language in which Buddhist teachings were first given and written down. See Chapter Three, Note 2, for more information.

CHAPTER TWO

1. See Gloria Mark's and colleagues' research: Mark, G., Gonzalez, V. M. & Harris, J., (2005) 'No Task Left Behind? Examining the Nature of Fragmented Work Proceedings of the Conference on Human Factors in Computing Systems', CHI 2005, Portland, Oregon, USA,

April 2–7 2005 doi:10.1145/1054972.1055017; Mark, G., Gudith, D. & Klocke, U. (2010), 'The Cost of Interrupted Work: More speed and Stress. Proceedings of the 2008 Conference on Human Factors in Computing Systems', CHI 2008, 2008, Florence, Italy, 5–10 April 2008, doi:10.1145/1357054.1357072

2. See Ruby Wax, *A Mindfulness Guide for the Frazzled* (Penguin, 2016) and *A Mindfulness Guide for Survival* (Welbeck, 2021).

3. Lisa Feldman Barrett, *How Emotions Are Made: The Secret Life of the Brain* (Pan Books, 2017).

4. For a review of this approach, see Andy Clark, *Surfing Uncertainty: Prediction, Action and the Embodied Mind* (Oxford University Press, 2016), Lawrence Barsalou (2008), 'Grounded cognition', *Annual Review of Psychology, 59*, pp. 617–45 and Lisa Feldman Barrett, *How Emotions Are Made: The Secret Life of the Brain* (Pan Books, 2017) and Manjaly, Z. M. & Iglesias, S. (2020), 'A computational theory of mindfulness based cognitive therapy from the "Bayesian brain" perspective', *Frontiers in Psychiatry*, 11, p. 404.

5. See Figure 4.1 in Feldman Barrett, L., *How Emotions Are Made* (Pan Books, 2017, p. 61).

CHAPTER THREE

1. Arthur P. Shimamura (2015), 'Muybridge in motion: travels in art, psychology and neurology', *History of Photography*, vol. 26, pp. 341–50.

2. Vedana was first translated as either 'sensation' or 'feeling', but scholars of early Buddhism have shown that it refers to the affective quality of anything that comes into contact with the body/mind – Peacock, J. & Batchelor, M. (2018), 'Vedana: What is in a "Feeling?"' *Contemporary Buddhism*, 19(1) pp. 1–6; Weber, A. M. (2018) 'Hedonic hotspots, hedonic potholes: *Vedanā* revisited', *Contemporary Buddhism*, 19, pp. 7–30; Williams, J. M. G., Baer, R., Batchelor, M., et al., (2022), 'What next after MBSR/MBCT: an open trial of an eight-week

follow-on program exploring mindfulness of feeling tone
(vedana)', *Mindfulness* doi.org/10.1007/s12671-022-01929-0

Interest in affective tone is not just one taking place in
psychology but also within philosophy. See, for example,
Barlassina, L. & Hayward, M. K. (2019) 'More of me! Less
of me!: Reflexive Imperativism about Affective Phenomenal
Character', *Mind*, 128, p. 512, October 2019.

3. From Joseph Goldstein (2005) 'Feelings: The Gateway to
    Liberation', talk 19 October 2005 at Insight Meditation
    Society, https://dharmaseed.org/talks/player/36199.html

4. Damasio, A., *The Strange Order of Things* (Vintage,
    Penguin, 2018).

5. This is the major finding of Nancy Bardacke and her colleagues
    in the field of mindfulness-based childbirth – they observe that
    many women miss those moments in labour when a contraction
    has eased because their minds are understandably drawn to
    the peak of the last contraction and fearfulness of the next. See
    Bardacke, N., *Mindful Birthing: Training the Mind, Body and
    Heart for Childbirth and Beyond* (Bravo Ltd, 2012).

6. Lisa Feldman Barrett, *How Emotions Are Made* (Macmillan,
    2017, p. 56).

7. Ibid p. 121.

CHAPTER FIVE

1. Baer, R., Crane, C., Miller, E. & Kuyken, W. (2019), 'Doing
    no harm in mindfulness-based programs: conceptual issues
    and empirical findings', *Clinical Psychology Review*, 71, pp.
    101–14, https://doi.org/10.1016/j.cpr.2019.01.001

2. We are grateful to David Treleaven for his advice on this
    section, and for his 2018 book *Trauma Sensitive Mindfulness:
    Practices for Safe and Transformative Healing* (W. W. Norton).

3. Singh, N. N., Singh, J., Singh, A. D. A., Singh, A. N. A. &
    Winton, A. S. W. (2011), 'Meditation on the soles of the feet for
    anger management: A trainer's manual', Raleigh, NC: Fernleaf
    (www.fernleafpub.com). In our Oxford Mindfulness Centre's

work in prisons, we have found that inmates appreciate a simple way of dealing with moods when things get too stressful, especially when they are about to get into arguments or fights.

4. Psychologist Nirbhay Singh pioneered this field and has taught the 'Soles of the Feet' technique successfully to school students: Selver, J. C. & Singh, N. N., *Mindfulness in the Classroom: An evidence-based program to reduce disruptive behavior and increase academic engagement* (Oakland, CA, New Harbinger, 2020); for adolescents with autism: Singh, N. N., Lancioni, G. E., Manikam, R., Winton, A. S. W., Singh, A. N. A., Singh, J. & Singh, A. D. A (2011), 'A mindfulness-based strategy self-management of aggressive behavior in adolescents with autism', *Research in Autism Spectrum Disorders*, 5, pp. 1153–8; adults with learning difficulties: Singh, N. N., Lancioni, G. E., Winton, A. S. W., Adkins, A. D., Singh, J. & Singh, A. N. (2007), 'Mindfulness training assists individuals with moderate mental retardation to maintain their community placements', *Behavior Modification*, 31, pp. 800–14; and older adults with Alzheimer's disease: Singh, N.N., Lancioni, G. E., Medvedev, O. N., Sreenivas, S., Myers, R. E. & Hwang, Y. (2018), 'Meditation on the Soles of the Feet Practice Provides Some Control of Aggression for Individuals with Alzheimer's Disease', *Mindfulness*, published online Dec. 2018, doi: 10.1007/s12671-018-1075-0; the Mindfulness in Schools Program uses a similar approach, inviting students to take a moment to feel their feet on the floor and their buttocks on the chair. The students named it FOFBOC (feet on floor, butt on chair); see www.mindfulnessinschools.org

5. R. S. Thomas, 'The Bright Field', *Collected Poems* (Phoenix, 1993, p.302).

6. We are grateful to Willoughby Britton for this distinction (International Conference on Mindfulness, Amsterdam, 13 July 2018).

CHAPTER SIX

1. Feldman Barrett, L., *How Emotions Are Made* (Pan Books, 2017, p. 58).

2. We are grateful to meditation teacher Ajahn Samedho for these helpful phrases.

3. Lippelt, D. P., Hommel, B. & Colzato, L. S. (2014), 'Focused attention, open monitoring and loving kindness meditation: effects on attention, conflict monitoring, and creativity – A review', *Frontiers in Psychology*, 5, article no. 1083, doi: 10.3389/fpsyg.2014.01083

4. Kerr, C., Sacchet, M. D., Lazar, S. W., Moore, C.I. & Jones, S.R., 'Mindfulness starts with the body: somatosensory attention and top-down modulation of cortical alpha rhythms in mindfulness meditation', *Frontiers in Human Neuroscience*, 7., article no. 12., doi: 10.3389/fnhum.2013.00012

5. Roiser et al. (2012), 'Cognitive mechanisms of treatment in depression', *Neuropharmacology*, 37, pp. 117–36.

6. Pasto, L. & Burack J. (2002), 'Visual filtering and focusing among persons with schizophrenia, major depressive disorder and no psychiatric history', *Canadian Journal of Behavioural Science*, 34, pp. 239–49.

7. Dietl, T., et al (2001), 'Enhanced long-latency somatosensory potentials in MDD', *Journal of Psychiatric Research*, 35, pp. 43–8.

8. Kemp et al. (2009), 'Fronto-temporal alteration within the first 200ms during an attentional task distinguished MDD, non-clinical participants with depressed mood and healthy controls', *Human Brain Mapping*, 30, pp. 602–14.

9. Hasenkamp, W., Wilson-Mendenhall, C. D., Duncan, E. & Barsalou, L. W. (2012), 'Mind wandering and attention during focused meditation: a fine-grained temporal analysis of fluctuating cognitive states', *Neuroimage*, 59, pp. 750–60, doi: 10.1016/j.neuroimage.2011.07.008

10. e.g. Tang, Y. Y., Qilin, L., Gen, X., Stein, E. A., Yang, Y. & Posner, M. I. (2010), 'Short-term meditation induces

white matter changes in the anterior cingulate', *Proc.
Nat. Acad. Sci. U.S.A.* 107, pp. 15649–52, doi: 10.1073/
pnas.1011043107

11.   Mrazek, Michael D., Franklin, Michael S., Phillips, Dawa
Tarchin, Baird, Benjamin & Schooler, Jonathan W. (2013),
'Mindfulness training improves working memory capacity
and GRE performance while reducing mind wandering',
Psychological Science, 24(5), pp. 776–81.

CHAPTER SEVEN

1.   The original research was done by Loftus, E. F. & Palmer, J. C.
(1974), 'Reconstruction of automobile destruction: an example
of the interaction between language and memory', *Journal
of Verbal Learning and Verbal Behavior,* 13, pp. 585–9. A
good summary of this research can be found at https://www.
simplypsychology.org/loftus-palmer.html#:~:text=Loftus

2.   Although the words you use to describe unpleasantness may
be different to those used by others, and may vary from
time to time, learning to make such distinctions increases
your emotional awareness and also leads to greater overall
wellbeing: Eckland, N. S. & Berenbaum, H. (2021), 'Emotional
awareness in daily life: exploring its potential role in repetitive
thinking and healthy coping', *Behavior Therapy*, https://doi.
org/10.1016/j.beth.2020.04.010; Starr, L. R., Hershenberg,
R., Shaw, Z. A., Li, Y. I. & Santee, A. C. (2020), 'The perils
of murky emotions: emotion differentiation moderates the
prospective relationship between naturalistic stress exposure
and adolescent depression', *Emotion*, 20 (6); Liu, D. Y., Gilbert,
K. E. & Thompson, R. J. (2020), 'Emotion differentiation
moderates the effects of rumination on depression: a
longitudinal study', *Emotion*, 20(7), pp. 1234–43.

3.   If you have tinnitus, it might be difficult to focus on sounds
when in a quiet room. Feel free to find an alternative to sounds
for this part of the meditation (for example, focusing instead on
sensations in the body or opening eyes and seeing objects in or

outside the room, using these to register pleasant/unpleasant). Having said this, if you are willing to stay for a little while with tinnitus, sometimes it can reveal new things about what is generating the sense of unpleasant: the noise itself or the (understandable) frustration and other feelings and thoughts created by the noise.

4. Torre, J. B. and Lieberman, M.D. (2018), 'Putting feelings into words: affect labeling as implicit emotion regulation', *Emotion Review*, 10, pp. 116–24.

5. Kircanski, K., Lieberman, M. D. & Craske, M.G. (2012), 'Feelings into words: contributions of language to exposure therapy', *Psychological Science*, 21 (10), pp. 1086–091; Lieberman, M. D., Eisenberger, N. I., Crockett, M. J., Tom, S. M., Pfeifer, J. H. & Way, B. M. (2007), 'Putting feelings into words: affect labeling disrupts amygdala activity to affective stimuli', *Psychological Science*, 18:421–8, doi:10.1111/j.1467-9280.2007.01916.x. [PubMed: 17576282]; Lieberman, M. D., Inagaki, T. K., Tabibnia, G. and Crockett, M. J. (2011), 'Subjective responses to emotional stimuli during labeling, reappraisal, and distraction', *Emotion*, 3:468–80, doi:10.1037/a0023503.[PubMed: 21534661]

6. Creswell, J. D., Way, B. M., Eisenberger, N. I. & Lieberman, M. D. (2007), 'Neural correlates of dispositional mindfulness during affect labeling', *Psychosomatic Medicine*, 69(6), pp. 560–65.

CHAPTER EIGHT

1. Psychologist Filip Raes and colleagues at the University of Leuven use a questionnaire that asks how you respond when you feel happy, excited or enthused. They found that people who react to positive mood by saying to themselves such things as, 'I remind myself these feelings won't last', 'I think about things that could go wrong' or, 'I don't deserve this' are at greater risk of more serious depression. Raes, F., Smets, J., Nelis. S. & Schoofs, H. (2012), 'Dampening of positive affect

prospectively predicts depressive symptoms in non-clinical samples', *Cognition & Emotion*, 26(1), pp. 75–82. For the questionnaire, see Feldman, G. C., Joorman, J., & Johnson, S. L. (2008), 'Responses to positive affect: a self-report measure of rumination and dampening', *Cognitive Therapy & Research*, 32(4), pp. 507–525.

2. These are called meta-emotions (an emotion about an emotion, such as feeling guilty about being irritable). It is helpful to look out for them as they can wind up creating even more depression. Bailen, N. H., Wu, H. & Thompson, R. J. (2019), 'Meta-emotions in daily life: associations with emotional awareness and depression', *Emotion*, 19(5), pp. 776–87.

3. This was the insight that motivated Jon Kabat-Zinn to offer mindfulness to chronic-pain patients in the clinic he set up in the University of Massachusetts Medical Center in 1979. The first formal practice for these patients, the Body Scan, invited participants to become aware of their bodies. This seems exactly the opposite of what one might think such patients need. Weren't they already too aware of their pain? But Jon Kabat-Zinn realised that thoughts and emotions about the pain had become inextricably entangled with the body sensations themselves. Bringing kindly awareness to the body helped to disentangle the knots as the thoughts and harsh judgments and emotions could be seen, held in a larger space and uncoupled from each other. See Jon Kabat-Zinn *Full Catastophe Living: Using the Wisdom of Your Body and Mind to Face Stress, Pain and Illness* (second edition, Bantam Books, 2013).

4. Birch, V. & Penman, D., *Mindfulness for Health: A practical guide to relieving pain, reducing stress and restoring well-being* (Piatkus, 2013); see also Gordon., A. & Ziv, A., *The Way Out: The revolutionary scientifically proven approach to heal chronic pain* (Vermilion, 2021).

5. Nancy Bardacke, *Mindful Birthing: Training the mind, body and heart for childbirth and beyond* (HarperOne, 2012).

6. See review of evidence in Warriner, S., Crane, C., Dymond, M. & Krusche, A. (2018), 'An evaluation of mindfulness-based

childbirth and parenting courses for pregnant women and prospective fathers/partners within the UK NHS (MBCP-4-NHS)', *Midwifery*, 64, pp. 1–10; see also Veringa-Skiba, I. K., de Bruin, E. I., van Steensel, F. J. A., & Bögels, S. M. (2022), 'Fear of childbirth, non-urgent obstetric interventions, and newborn outcomes: a randomized controlled trial comparing Mindfulness-Based Childbirth and Parenting with enhanced care as usual', *Birth*, 49(1), 40–51. https://doi.org/10.1111/birt.12571

7. Rachman, S. & DeSilva, P. de (1978), 'Abnormal and normal obsessions', *Behaviour Research & Therapy*, 16, pp. 233–48. These authors found that such thoughts and impulses are normal. They include the impulse to physically and verbally attack someone, having a sexual impulse towards another person, to jump on the rails when a train is approaching or the impulse to say rude and unacceptable things to someone. On average, people report recognising between one and three such thoughts or impulses having passed through their mind at some point during any week.

8. For people who struggle with addictions, psychiatrist and mindfulness teacher Jud Brewer has explored how mindfulness of feeling tones can help. For instance, for those addicted to cigarettes – he invites people to really focus on the taste of the cigarette itself as it is being smoked. Many of his participants say that they realised for the first time that they don't actually *like* the taste of it. He and his team have produced books and apps that can be used to help with addictions, and there is good evidence for their effectiveness. See Brewer, J., *The Craving Mind From Cigarettes to Smartphones to Love: Why we get hooked and how we can break bad habits* (Yale University Press, 2018).

9. Hanson, R., *Hardwiring Happiness: How to reshape your brain and your life* (Rider, 2014).

CHAPTER NINE

1. *Northern Lights* is published as *The Golden Compass* in the USA, Canada and several other countries.
2. Pullman, P., 'Poco a poco: The fundamental particles of narrative', in *Daemon Voices: On Stories and Storytelling* (David Fickling Books, 2017).
3. Pullman, P., 'Poco a poco: The fundamental particles of narrative', in *Daemon Voices: On Stories and Storytelling* (David Fickling Books, 2017, page 208).
4. Tipper, S. (2010), 'From observation to action simulation: the role of attention, eye-gaze, emotion, and body state', *Quarterly Journal of Experimental Psychology*, 63 (11), pp. 2081–2105.
5. Tucker, M. & Ellis, R. (1998), 'On the relations between seen objects and components of potential actions', *Journal of Experimental Psychology: Human Perception and Performance*, 24, pp. 830–46.
6. See Barsalou, L. W., Simmons, W. K., Barbey, A. K. & Wilson, C. D. (2003), 'Grounding conceptual knowledge in modality-specific systems', *Trends in Cognitive Sciences*, 7, pp. 84–91; and Barsalou, L. W. (2008), 'Grounded cognition', *Annual Review of Psychology*, 59, 617–45.
7. Pulvermüller, F. (2005), 'Brain mechanisms linking language and action', *Nature Reviews Neuroscience*, 6 (7) pp. 576–82.
8. For a review of this field's impact on our understanding of emotional problems, see Gjelsvik, B., Lovic, D. & Williams, J. M. G. (2018), 'Embodied cognition and emotional disorders: embodiment and abstraction in understanding depression', *Journal of Experimental Psychopathology*, July–September, pp. 1–41, doi: 10.5127/pr.035714
9. Schuch, S., Bayliss, A. P., Klein, C. & Tipper, S. P. (2010), 'Attention modulates motor system activation during action observation: evidence for inhibitory rebound', *Experimental Brain Research*, 205(2), pp. 235–49, https://doi.org/10.1007/s00221-010-2358-4
10. The brain activity while watching the video was followed

rapidly by a change in the reverse direction to stop the actual action itself.

11. Barsalou, L. W., *Situated Simulation in the Human Conceptual System* (Elsevier, 2003).

12. Blakemore, S. J. & Decety, J. (2001), 'From the perception of action to the understanding of intention', *Nature Reviews Neuroscience*, 2, pp. 561–7.

13. Elgendi, M., et al. (2018), 'Subliminal Priming – State of the Art and Future Perspectives', *Behavioral Sciences*, 8, 54.

14. In addition, the prime is usually followed by a 'pattern mask' – a jumbled word that appears in the place where the prime appeared. This makes sure the volunteer is unaware of what the prime word was.

15. Fazio, R. H., Sanbonmatsu, D. M., Powell, M. C. & Kardes, F. R. (1986), 'On the automatic activation of attitudes', *Journal of Personality and Social Psychology*, 50, pp. 229–38.

16. Feldman Barrett, L., *How Emotions Are Made: The Secret Life of the Brain* (MacMillan, 2017); see pp.118–27 and Appendix D, p. 313ff.

17. Crane, C., Jandric, D., Barnhofer, T. & Williams, J. M. G. (2010), 'Dispositional mindfulness, meditation and conditional goal setting', *Mindfulness*, 1, pp. 204–14.

CHAPTER TEN

1. Robert N. Buck, *Weather Flying* (A & C Black, 1970).

2. Buck, Robert O. Preface to 5th edition of *Weather Flying*. Robert N. Buck and Robert O. Buck (McGraw Hill, 2013), page xv.

3. This was one of the early visits made by Mark Williams, with colleagues John Teasdale and Zindel Segal to the Centre for Mindfulness at UMass as they were developing MBCT, as told in their book: Segal., Z. V., Williams, J. M. G. & Teasdale, J. D., *Mindfulness-based Cognitive Therapy for Depression* (2002), second edition, Guilford Press, 2013, pp. 53 and 57–8.

4. We are grateful to meditation teacher Christina Feldman for this guidance.

5. Lim, D., Condon, P. & DeSteno, D. (2015), 'Mindfulness and compassion: an examination of mechanism and scalability', *PloS one*, *10*(2), e0118221, https://doi.org/10.1371/journal.pone.0118221

6. Meland, A., Hoebeke, E., Pensgaard, A. M., Fonne, V., Wagstaff, A. & Jensen, C. G. (2021), 'A Sense of Fellowship: Mindfulness improves experienced interpersonal benefits and prosociality in a military aviation unit', *International Journal of Aerospace Psychology*, doi: 10.1080/24721840.2020.1865818; Donald, J. N., Sahdra, B. K., van Zanden, B., Duineveld, J. J., Atkins, P.W.B., Marshall, S. L. & Ciarrochi, J. (2019), 'Does your mindfulness benefit others? A systematic review and meta-analysis of the link between mindfulness and prosocial behaviour', *British Journal of Psychology*, 110, pp. 101–25.

CHAPTER ELEVEN

1. Steel, P. (2007), 'The nature of procrastination: a meta-analytic and theoretical review of quintessential self-regulatory failure, *Psychological Bulletin*, 133(1), pp. 65–94, doi:10.1037/0033-2909.133.1.65; Prem, R., Scheel, T. E., Weigelt, O., Hoffmann, K. & Korunka, C. (2018), 'Procrastination in daily working life: a diary study on within-person processes that link work characteristics to workplace procrastination', *Frontiers in Psychology*, 9:1087, doi:10.3389/fpsyg.2018.01087

2. Research has shown that if you ask volunteers to do a task while ignoring distractors, then the stimuli used as distractors are rated afterwards as less pleasant, and if photos of human faces were used as distractors, they are rated as less trustworthy. Raymond, J. E., Fenske, M. J. & Westoby, N. (2005), 'Emotional Devaluation of Distracting Patterns and Faces: A Consequence of Attentional Inhibition During Visual Search?' *Journal of Experimental Psychology: Human*

Perception and Performance, 31(6), pp. 1404–15, https://doi.org/10.1037/0096-1523.31.6.1404

3. See Note 1.

4. Ferrari, J., Johnson, J. & McCown, W., *Procrastination and Task Avoidance – Theory, Research and Treatment* (Springer Science+Business Media, 1995), doi: 10.1007/978-1-4899-0227-6

5. Bhalla, M. & Proffitt, D. R. (1999), 'Visual–motor recalibration in geographical slant perception', *Journal of Experimental Psychology: Human Perception and Performance,* 25(4), pp. 1076–96.

6. We are grateful to our colleague Sarah Silverton, senior mindfulness teacher and author of *The Mindfulness Key* (2012), for permission to use this practice in Week Seven.

CHAPTER TWELVE

1. See 'The mere presence of your smartphone reduces brain power' at https://www.sciencedaily.com/releases/2017/06/170623133039.htm

2. Al-Mosaiwi, M. & Johnstone, T. (2018), 'In an absolute state: elevated use of absolutist words is a marker specific to anxiety, depression, and suicidal ideation', *Clinical Psychological Science,* 6, pp. 529–42.

3. If a therapy is to be effective in reducing risk of future depression, whether cognitive therapy or mindfulness-based cognitive therapy – or, indeed, vedana – then it needs to cultivate this skill; see Farb, N., Anderson, A., Ravindran, A., Hawley, L., Irving, J., Mancuso, E., Gulamani, T., Williams, G., Ferguson, A. & Segal, Z. V. (2018), 'Prevention of relapse/recurrence in major depressive disorder with either mindfulness-based cognitive therapy or cognitive therapy', *Journal of Consulting and Clinical Psychology,* 86(2), pp. 200–4.

ACKNOWLEDGEMENTS

This book, and the programme it contains, would not have come together if it were not for the help and support of many people. We are grateful for the advice and guidance on the science from colleagues Alan Baddeley, Tim Dalgleish, Barney Dunn, Martin Eimer, Elaine Fox, Bergljot Gjelsvik, Dirk Hermans, Filip Raes and Steve Tipper. Nor could we have done this without the advice and guidance on the early Buddhist background from John Peacock, Catherine McGee, Martine Batchelor, Helen Ma and Chris Cullen. We are also grateful to Robert Williams for keeping us up to date with the philosophy that is also exploring the affective tone of experience.

The first major exploration of how these meditations might help deepen and sustain mindfulness practice was with Helen Ma, who co-taught alongside Mark Williams for several years in training retreats offered as part of the Foundations Course for Teaching Mindfulness-based Cognitive Therapy in Hong Kong, and much of the framing and language of the eventual programme was deeply influenced by her wisdom and kindness.

As the programme emerged from retreat to a more 'mainstream' context, the Wheatley Mindfulness Network were willing to undertake a prototype six-session version of the programme, and we are grateful to Roger Bettess, Jen Yeates, Christine Bainbridge, Tom Goss, Lonnie Gross, Julian Gross, Ann Gajda, Norbert Gajda, Elaine Parsons, Tanya Berman, Frances Simpson, Caroline Sants, Celia Montague, Bob Webster, Liz Barry, Tony Barry, Juliet Vale, Hilary Wright, Pat Jeffs and Polly Jeffs.

In these early stages of developing the course, colleagues Rebecca Crane, Ee-Lin Ong, Helen Ma, Chris Cullen, Andy Phee, Melanie Fennell, Johannes Michalak and Thomas Heidenreich gave further feedback on drafts of the programme, and David Treleaven gave wise advice that helped develop the course in a way that would take account of the trauma that many participants have faced in the past. It helped us greatly that Rebecca Crane and the Rowen Mindfulness Group in North Wales, as well as colleagues in Hong Kong and China, were willing to try out the meditations at an early stage and offer feedback which helped to inform the final programme.

We were delighted that teacher/trainer colleagues from the Institute for Mindfulness South Africa (IMISA) were willing to work through the pilot progamme and give feedback: Matthew Watkin, Barbara Gerber, Anneke Barnard, Craig Henen, Danielle Klemp, Denise Washkansky, Fathima Bux, Ashika Pillay, Janine Kirby, Julie Deane-Williams, Linda Kantor, Mandy Johnson, Nico Brink, RJ Chippindall, Simon Whitesman, Debbie Grusd, Luke Younge and Kate Leinberger.

And we are especially grateful to IMISA trainers Matthew Watkin, Mandy Johnson, Linda Kantor, Barbara Gerber and Janine Kirby who, alongside Ee-Lin Ong (New Zealand) and Andy Phee (UK), taught the full eight-week programme to participant volunteers in an open research trial to evaluate it. The research itself would not have been possible without the research team in Oxford – Emma Medlicott, Kath de Wilde, Lucy Radley and Laura Taylor – who worked on the trial from start to finish, from securing ethics permission to setting up files for data, conducting the data analysis and being core members of the write-up team, alongside Ruth Baer, John Peacock and Chris Cullen. Special thanks go to the participants in the research trial in South Africa, New Zealand and the UK, who gave us wonderful and detailed descriptions of their experiences as they journeyed through the eight-week course – most in the midst of the pandemic – and allowed us to use their experiences to inform this book, to the benefit of others.

We are grateful to teachers and staff at the Oxford Mindfulness Centre (OMC) who continue to support the dissemination of the programme. Thanks go to Willem Kuyken, Alison and Peter Yiangou, Claire Kelly and Sharon Hadley, and all the wonderful OMC teacher/trainers who are now teaching the programme. The OMC was particularly helpful in encouraging us to put together an on-line 'taster' version of the course during 2021, and participants from eighty-two countries took part and were able to give helpful feedback.

In bringing the book together, we thank Sarah Silverton for permission to use her Week 7 practice. Thanks also to Pat Simpson and Beth MacKay for permission to use their stories and experiences. These, in keeping with all the stories and experiences included in the book, have been anonymised and altered to preserve anonymity. We are grateful to Jen Williams, who read and commented on the first draft of the text.

We remain enormously grateful to Sheila Crowley at Curtis Brown, Kris Dahl at ICM Partners, to Zoe Bohm, Jillian Stewart, Matt Crossey and Holly Harley at Piatkus, and to Nana Twumasi and Natalie Bautista at Hachette.

Finally, each of us owes a tremendous debt to our partners, Phyllis and Bella, and our children, Rob, Jen and Annie and Sasha and Luka, for their love, patience and support throughout the preoccupation with the inevitable challenges of writing.

INDEX